TRANSFORMATIONAL
LIVING
Discover Your Kingdom Assignment

RANDY R. BUTLER

Copyright © 2024 Mission Increase.

ISBN (Hardcover): 979-8-9906208-3-4
ISBN (Paperback): 979-8-9906208-2-7
ISBN (E-book): 979-8-9906208-4-1

Attention: Permissions Coordinator
Mission Increase Publishing
12909 SW 68th Pkwy
#455 Portland, OR 97223
info@missionincrease.org

This book follows the pattern of Bible translations like the English Standard Version, the Christian Standard Bible, and the New International Version in not capitalizing pronouns referring to God. Names and titles of God are capitalized.

Praise for *Transformational Living: Discover Your Kingdom Assignment*

"Dr. Randy Butler's Transformational Living: Discover Your Kingdom Assignment offers profound insights that are both inspiring and practical. This book is a must-read for anyone seeking to lead a life of purpose and impact, grounded in deep spiritual wisdom and love of Christ."

Dr. Ron Post, Founder
Medical Teams International

"I discovered Transformational Living at a time when I was searching for a resource to help guide a group of fellow believers into a journey of deeper faith and generous stewardship. Through it we found more than inspirational ideas; we discovered a detailed roadmap for how to walk the journey of discipleship together in an engaging and memorable way. What we started together will endure into the far future."

Rev. Dr. Ben Lee, President
In His Steps Foundation

"My wife and I took part in a Transformational Living Weekend at a low time when we were

searching for God's clear direction in our lives. We knew we wanted to be good stewards of what He'd entrusted to us, but to consider a Kingdom Business Plan for our lives? We'd never processed our future from that perspective, and it brought great clarity, inspiration, and hope for the road ahead."

Lee Wilhite
Chief Operations Officer
Mission Increase

artifacts photos are from the author's personal collection. Used with permission.

For information about scheduling an in-person workshop with Randy Butler or ordering the *Transformational Living: Discover Your Kingdom Assignment* group study package, please visit missionincrease.org/transformational-living.

Printed in the United States of America.

TABLE OF CONTENTS

AUTHOR THANKS

Special thanks to Marty Duren for taking my spoken words and putting them to paper, as well as his contributions of editing and content creation in the Workbook and Leader's Guide of this study.

Special thanks to Caleb Crider for managing the *Transformational Living: Discover Your Kingdom Assignment* project to the finish line.

FOREWORD

I have been fascinated all my life with economic innovation and God's created order. Even as a boy I read business magazines that arrived at our home from cover to cover to learn about mankind's unceasing desire to innovate product design, manufacturing techniques, and materials science. Adam Smith noted that society at large benefited from such "selfish" profit-making impulses as if by an invisible hand. I continue to marvel at this dynamic and reading about it is still thrilling to me in my sixties.

Man's capacity to create and to innovate is a consequence of having been made in the image of God, who spoke the universe into existence. The fact that the five famous American nineteenth century innovators discussed in this book were actively exploring their own relationship with the God of the Bible is only a surprise to me because of the generally harsh treatment they have received at the hands of historians. My studies through the years point to America's rich legacy of philanthropy being rooted in the generosity of these men and others who imitated them. As a student of biblical generosity, it is clear that America has no rival in this space. Americans are charitable and this impulse is closely related to our country's origins in natural law and the Judeo-Christian consensus that was in place at the time of its founding.

I met Randy through a dynamic capacity building ministry called Mission Increase. I have also heard him share these same ideas from the dais at the Free Market Forum, an annual event dedicated to exploring the nexus of markets and morality sponsored by Hillsdale College and Acton Institute.

Transformational Living: Discover Your Kingdom Assignment is helpful because it points the way for the current generation to graft into this same rich tradition. Ephesians 2:10 declares that we were saved "unto good works which God prepared in advance for us to walk in." Tim Keller's book *Center Church* is one in this growing genre of texts that argues for marketplace Christians to elevate their game. For the church to be the church (the Greek word *ecclesia* or "called out ones") it needs to revert to the revolutionary movement that began on the cross and that is intended by God to be 24/7/365—a movement and not an institution.

Galatians 3:28 says that in Christ we are all one. The major cleavages of society during Christ's short time on earth—gender, slave/free, Jew/Gentile—were meaningless relative to the unity that is only possible in Christ. In Jesus' high priestly prayer in John 17, He prays that we all might be one. If we heed Paul's exhortation in Colossians 3 to take all thoughts captive to Christ, we will see more things on earth as they are in Heaven. This was the impulse that shaped the America that Alexis de Tocqueville observed and recorded in his 1837 classic, *Democracy in America*. When Americans reclaim their full citizenship in the kingdom of God, twenty-first century America will once again be noted by observers around the world for its exceptionalism. America was exceptional because its people attempted to imitate the God of the Bible. A great many Americans over the centuries have chosen to imitate God in his generosity of time, talent, treasure, and testimony. I am thanking God that Randy Butler has invested all four of his T's in this important new book. May God be glorified as you read it and take its lessons to heart. God help us to not only be hearers of the Word, but also doers.

David A. Durell, Chairman
The George Edward Durell Foundation

INTRODUCTION

Welcome to *Transformational Living: Discover Your Kingdom Assignment*. My name is Randy Butler. I am a pastor, a parent, a spouse, and an historian. I work with a faith-based nonprofit called Mission Increase. We come alongside leaders in the Christian nonprofit space, helping them become more effective in creating financial stability for their organizations so the organization can remain laser-focused on its mission. Such a focus happens when people become aware of what God is calling them to do with their lives; a calling I refer to as our Kingdom Assignment.

Our Kingdom Assignment is not something we dream up on our own. Like salvation, our Kingdom Assignment isn't given to us through any earthly means. It is literally the role that God has picked out for us, so we can accomplish in his kingdom what he wants from each and every one of his children.

The book you are now reading results from years of study and observation as I've watched God change people's lives who have implemented these principles. Be assured this isn't a "self-help" book that simply tries to help you be a better version of the current you. We don't merely need better versions of ourselves; we need to be transformed by God, *day by day as we live*.

Dropping Your Burden

How often do you feel overwhelmed with the struggles and challenges of life? Sometimes? Often? All the time? I think I have some very good news for you. Discovering your Kingdom Assignment can be like a breath of fresh air, a weight off one's shoulders, or a newfound freedom from bondage. This way of living brings peace, purpose, meaning, and great joy.

How do you discover your Kingdom Assignment? God will show it to you as a result of him transforming your life to be more like Jesus. I call it Transformational Living because that's what it is: God transforming me and using me in some small way to transform others.

I didn't invent this way of living. No amount of human expertise could have invented such a transformation. This really should come as no surprise since, according to Isaiah 55:8–9, "His ways are not our ways and his thoughts are not our thoughts." This way of living is supernatural. In fact, I continue to discover more about it as I walk with Jesus.

How to Best Use This Book

I've attempted to write this book conversationally as though you and I are speaking to each other. Even if we don't know each other we still might have things in common. My hope is that as you read, it will feel as if we are in comfortable, familiar surroundings, enjoying a mug of coffee or tea, and talking about things that matter.

That doesn't mean you have to plunge into Transformational Living alone. By no means! While you can do so—and benefit from it—you will probably grow more if you read through it with someone who knows you well. Then set aside time for discussing what God teaches you in each chapter. God often uses brothers and sisters in Christ to sharpen and guide us, as well as helping us determine his will for our lives.

Transformational Living: Discover Your Kingdom Assignment is ten short chapters. We begin each chapter with a brief exploration of a passage of Scripture. Then, we will think through some possible implications of that passage to our lives. We will conclude each chapter with a call for personal reflection and for you to explore how you might walk faithfully with Jesus as he transforms your life and the lives of others through you.

Be sure to take notes as you read so you can refer to them during your discussion time. To have the fullest learning experience consider getting a copy of the *Transformational Living: Discover Your Kingdom Assignment Workbook*, which includes notes, discussion questions, and a scripture reading guide. (You can find ordering information as well as links to online teaching videos in the back of this book.)

Because this book is intended to make a difference in your life, you can be sure the evil one will bring distractions your way. Let me encourage you to be mindful of the importance of this material and strive to designate time each day for reading and reflection. When you read, put your phone in another room; put your computer to sleep; turn off the TV or streaming device; don't listen to music with lyrics so your brain won't be trying to process the written word and sung word at the same time. This is a time for concentration and hearing what the Spirit has to say to you.

Don't be surprised to find this just might be hard work, but if you put in the time and work hard, I believe you will reap the eternal benefits of doing God's work.

Getting Started

Several years ago, I watched a television series on The History Channel that God used to change my life. *The Men*

Who Built America was originally a six-part docuseries on the lives of five great American industrialists: Cornelius Vanderbilt, John D. Rockefeller, Andrew Carnegie, J.P. Morgan, and Henry Ford. As I watched *The Men Who Built America*, I was inspired to read more deeply about each of these men. I read countless pages of biographies, journals, notes, and historical documents. What I found was the History Channel had missed a significant part of the lives of the Industrialists: the influence of their faith in Jesus on their business dealings, their families, their community involvement, and church life. (I've included a Recommended Reading list on pages 149–151 for everyone interested in a deep-dive into their lives.)

John D. Rockefeller was a Baptist Sunday School superintendent and Board member who studied God's word and faithfully took his family to church each Sunday. Vanderbilt came to faith in Christ later in life resulting in a newfound generosity. Although he came to understand his Kingdom Assignment late, he nonetheless fulfilled what God had in mind for him in those remaining years.

Andrew Carnegie memorized two verses from the Psalms each day for school assignments. His writings contain scripture allusions and references to God's kingdom. J.P. Morgan was an outstanding church leader who invested his time, talent, and treasure in the life of the Episcopal church he attended in New York City. But it is his testimony through his will that is the guiding light:

I commit my soul into the hands of my Saviour, in full confidence that having redeemed it and washed it in His most precious blood He will present it faultless before my Heavenly Father; and I entreat my children to maintain and defend, at all hazard and at any cost of personal sacrifice, the blessed doctrine of the complete atonement for sin through the blood of Jesus Christ, once offered, and through that alone.

The fifth and last industrialist featured in the History Channel series is Henry Ford. Ford is most well-known for his implementation of the moving assembly line and development of systems for the mass production of automobiles. Ford's father was invested in the life of his church and influenced Henry, having the young Ford baptized and confirmed. This influence is noticeable at various times in Henry Ford's adulthood, though perhaps less obviously than the other four industrialists. In fact, my use of these industrialists isn't meant to lionize them or imply they were without fault. Each, like all of us, had his own struggles and flaws.

This brings us to our Kingdom Assignment. While the industrialists' lives deal with church, commerce, communities, cities, capitalism, and cars, what is your Kingdom Assignment? God has an assignment for each one of us today. It's important for us to know that that assignment is important to God. It needs to be discovered by you and me, then shared with others. This is very real. This is very important.

And it is needed for such a time as this.

Chapter One

ARE WE READY FOR HEAVEN?

For many people heaven is a matter of what matters most to them. Get to see their beloved grandmother? They think that's heaven. Get out from under an overbearing boss? They think that's heaven. Get to see and play with their favorite pet from childhood again? They think that's heaven. It's easy to see that most people have a conception of heaven that doesn't even require the presence of God. It's just a version of their preferred life on earth and nothing more.

But, that isn't the idea portrayed in the Bible. Heaven is a place. It's the dwelling place of God and God decides who enters and who doesn't. On one level, there is salvation readiness. On another level, there is Kingdom Assignment completion readiness.

This demands a question for all of us. It's perhaps the most important question in our lives: Are we ready for Heaven? Am I ready? Are you?

Being Prepared

The gospel of Matthew records an extended section of Jesus' teaching just prior to his death. Chapters 24 and 25 record his words about what happen before Jesus' return. If we read these prophecies correctly, we find great reasons for optimism about Christ's return. The Parable of the Fig Tree teaches us to be ready for Jesus. For those who know Jesus, being ready for him to come back for us is a source of continual encouragement!

Following the Parable of the Fig Tree, in Matthew 25, we find one of Jesus' teachings known as the Parable of the Talents. It reads:

> *"For it will be like a man going on a journey, who called his servants and entrusted to them his property. To one he gave five talents, to another two, to another one, to each according to his ability. Then he went away. He who had received*

the five talents went at once and traded with them, and he made five talents more. So also he who had the two talents made two talents more. But he who had received the one talent went and dug in the ground and hid his master's money. Now after a long time the master of those servants came and settled accounts with them. And he who had received the five talents came forward, bringing five talents more, saying, 'Master, you delivered to me five talents; here, I have made five talents more.' His master said to him, 'Well done, good and faithful servant. You have been faithful over a little; I will set you over much. Enter into the joy of your master.' And he also who had the two talents came forward, saying, 'Master, you delivered to me two talents; here, I have made two talents more.' His master said to him, 'Well done, good and faithful servant. You have been faithful over a little; I will set you over much. Enter into the joy of your master.' He also who had received the one talent came forward, saying, 'Master, I knew you to be a hard man, reaping where you did not sow, and gathering where you scattered no seed, so I was afraid, and I went and hid your talent in the ground. Here, you have what is yours.' But his master answered him, 'You wicked and slothful servant! You knew that I reap where I have not sown and gather where I scattered no seed?

Then you ought to have invested my money with the bankers, and at my coming I should have received what was my own with interest. So take the talent from him and give it to him who has the ten talents. For to everyone who has will more be given, and he will have an abundance. But from the one who has not, even what he has will be taken away. And cast the worthless servant into the outer darkness. In that place there will be weeping and gnashing of teeth.'" (vs 14–30, ESV)

It's clear the landowner gave to each of his servants an assignment to handle in his absence. Since this is a parable of the kingdom of God, we can call these responsibilities their Kingdom Assignments. Each of them was to invest a specific amount of money and manage it for the owner. If they managed well, they would be rewarded; if not, they would be judged. The landowner's expectation was clear by the two he called "good and faithful" servants. They were the ones who did his will; they completed their Kingdom Assignments.

We should notice something else in this parable: there is a sense of urgency. It says "immediately." What God would have us do for his kingdom is not something for us to care about a year from now or ten years from now. It is not something for us to care for if we're young or when we're old. This is not something—if we're still working—to care for when we move into retirement. The time is *now*. It is urgent that we learn and live out our Kingdom Assignment.

(We'll look at urgency more in depth later as well as two other important topics we see in the parable: leverage and stewardship.)

Your Kingdom Assignment and Others

Directly following the Parable of the Talents, Jesus shifts into a teaching about the final judgment. This teaching in Matthew 25:31–46 is sometimes referred to as the Parable of the Sheep and the Goats, with the sheep being those in God's family and the goats outside it. This section of scripture includes the well-known exchange with those who stand for judgment during which Jesus reveals the many opportunities those being judged had to minister to him as they helped—or didn't help—people in need. "When did we ever see you hungry, thirsty, a stranger, naked, sick or in prison?" they ask. Both the righteous and unrighteous seem shocked; they don't remember encountering Jesus at all! Then Jesus tells them, "Insomuch as you did it for the least of these my brothers and sisters, you did it for me!"

It isn't possible to complete our Kingdom Assignment without impacting the lives of others, whether they are in the middle or on the margins, at the summit or in the

13

gutter. Our assignment isn't for the purpose of making us feel fulfilled, although it will. It's about having an impact in the lives of people around us. It's God using us to demonstrate his love and salvation to those we connect with outside our church life.

Regardless of where you live, the physically hungry are around you. The spiritually thirsty are around you. Strangers—those who don't know the culture, the country, or God—are around you. The poor and sick are around you. The imprisoned in body, in mind, and in spirit are around you. We don't always know immediately which of these are "brothers and sisters" so we'd do well to help all of them we can!

The Industrialists and Their Pastors

You might be surprised to learn the five previously mentioned industrialists were not unaware of biblical teachings. All of them were influenced by their pastors. Charles Deems was pastor and personal advisor to Cornelius Vanderbilt and was present when Vanderbilt was ushered into heaven. Fred Gates was a Baptist pastor and personal advisor to John Rockefeller. Henry Sloan Coffin was a pastor to Andrew Carnegie. He later became president of Union Theological Seminary (1926-1945).

William S. Rainsford was pastor and longtime friend of J.P. Morgan. Samuel Marquis was pastor and advisor to Henry Ford. In fact, following World War I, Marquis headed up Ford's Department of Education (later known as the sociological department for the Ford Motor Company), providing for the housing, medical, and financial needs of Ford employees. (In my collection of industrialist memorabilia is a 1918 Ford Motor Company phone directory. Marquis is listed in it. It is one of the most prized possessions in my collection.)

Given the small number of people who become billionaires it is likely your Kingdom Assignment won't be the subject of a future documentary series. However, there will still be rejoicing in heaven over one sinner who repents as a result of your witness to the good news of Jesus whether or not you make the History Channel!

But, before we continue examining what it means to make an impact for heaven, let's make sure you're ready for heaven yourself.

What About You?

Before the King gives you a Kingdom Assignment you must be in his kingdom. God doesn't hand out Kingdom Assignments to rebels but to the repentant. So, before we proceed, review your life and what you think of as your relationship with God Almighty, creator of heaven and earth.

15

Have you repented of your sins and placed your faith in Jesus Christ alone for salvation? Have you turned your allegiance from the kingdoms of this world to the kingdom of God? In one of Jesus' earliest sermons, recorded in the New Testament gospel of Mark, he proclaimed: "The time is fulfilled, and the kingdom of God is at hand; repent and believe in the gospel" (1:15). The *gospel* is the good news of the kingdom of God. It is good news of personal redemption to be sure, but it is also the fulfillment of God's kingdom promises.

All of us—every human being ever born—are born into sin (Romans 3:23). We are by nature children of wrath and enemies of God. We are rebels toward the true King and his kingdom. Left to our own devices, we will obtain the wages of our sin: death (Romans 6:23).

Thankfully, God had already prepared a way of salvation, through his son Jesus Christ (John 1:12). The Bible says, "For God so loved the world, that He gave His only begotten Son, that whoever believes in Him shall not perish, but have eternal life" (John 3:16). Jesus stands at your heart's door, knocking to enter (Revelation 3:20). This is a promise for everyone!

How do you know if you are ready for heaven? It depends on whether you have trusted Jesus. If you haven't, you can do so right now. Here's a prayer you can pray to ask Jesus to save you:

Lord,

I acknowledge that I am a sinner and cannot save myself. I realize my sin has separated me from you. Thank you for sending Jesus to die in my place. I believe that he died on the cross for my sins and that you raised him from the dead so I can have new life! Please come into my heart and help me to love and serve you with my whole life.

Amen.

Information book for patients at the Henry Ford Hospital which was financed by Henry and Clara Ford. The first patients were admitted on October 1, 1915.

Chapter Two

URGENCY

𝗂𝗂𝗂𝗂𝗂𝗂𝗂𝗂𝗂𝗂𝗂𝗂𝗂𝗂𝗂

John D. Rockefeller understood urgency.

He understood a sense of urgency in business. He understood urgency with his children. And he understood urgency with people in general.

You don't build a monopoly worth an estimated $1 Trillion in today's dollars[1] by dilly-dallying around. One doesn't control an entire industry by waiting for things to happen.

When I think of John Rockefeller's life in business, I think of the word URGENCY among several other key

---

1 - https://www.visualcapitalist.com/most-valuable-companies-all-time/

words that would describe the methodical way in which Rockefeller went about conducting the ministry of business. The word urgency may carry with it overtones of thoughts that could include *emergency*, *panic*, or *crisis*. For Rockefeller, these words would be often avoided because of how he would steward the word urgency.

Rockefeller played the "long game" with what I call "methodical urgency." An example, as Grace Goulder noted would be that, "His religion was a practical religion as befitted to a practical man. He used his Bible freely like a tool."[2]

For Rockefeller, the urgent was always the immediate, but he acted with great patience, even in his younger years. When young, he had the wisdom of a wise old man. When older, he had the courage of a young roaring lion: always looking for opportunities, always making the most of every opportunity, always drawing the net as to not miss the opportunity. This would be the life of Rockefeller living life with passionate urgency.

It's doubtful we would know the names of any of the Industrialists if they'd had no sense of urgency about their goals.

---

2 - Goulder, Grace. *John D. Rockefeller: The Cleveland Years*, (Cleveland: The Western Reserve Historical Society), 1972, p 45.

Kingdom Urgency

Do Christians need to have a sense of urgency about anything? To look at the average Christian is to see people who act like balloons on a breeze rather than rockets taking flight. The scriptures don't give us the option for passivity! They demand a sense of urgency. Consider Matthew 7:13–14, which reads, "Enter through the narrow gate; for the gate is wide and the way is broad that leads to destruction, and there are many who enter it. For the gate is small and the way is narrow that leads to life, and there are few who find it."

What could possibly be more urgent than making people aware of these two gates and two paths. There is a broad gate to avoid and a narrow gate to enter. These are eternal destinations! We can look around us each day and see people destroying their lives. There are those in our families, people we work with, friends and neighbors, and others in our orbits who are barreling head-long down the broad way to destruction.

They need someone to wave a flag, to warn them of impending doom. It is *urgent* they hear the gospel before it is too late.

New York City is one of my favorite places. Once while visiting, I took a walk down West Broadway. I looked up and saw a sign above a business that read, "The time is now." I was so impacted that I took a picture. I've never forgotten that simple slogan: The time is now.

Is there anything more true as you consider your Kingdom Assignment and develop your Kingdom Business Plan than living with the urgency your assignment requires? The time is not next week; the time is now!

People are lost, lonely, and hurting. Some are hungry; some are thirsty. Others are in prison or out on parole, struggling to find meaningful work and survive. Consider a few statistics about conditions in the United States to draw these thoughts into focus:

- 1-in-4 women and 1-in-4 men have experienced some form of physical violence by an intimate partner (National Coalition Against Domestic Violence)
- More than 600,000 children are abused each year (National Children's Alliance)
- More than half of all women and nearly 33% of all men have experienced sexual violence via contact during their lifetimes (CDC)
- In 2020, an estimated 14.8 million adults reported at least one major depressive episode in the previous year (ADAA)
- Nearly 38 million people are living in poverty (US Census Bureau)

- More than 1.2 million people are in US jails as of 2022, with numbers of both male and female inmates increasing (Bureau of Justice Statistics)
- Worldwide, more than 108 million individuals have been forcibly displaced due to persecution, conflict, violence, and human rights violations (World Vision)

And, tragically, in 2021 the number of Americans who have a religious membership fell below 50% for the first time (Gallup) with about 40 million dropping out of attendance in the last twenty-five years.[3]

With so much trauma and hurt, it is a great blessing that God can use us to help people find freedom in this life. In Luke 4:18–19, Jesus reads from the Old Testament book of Isaiah: "The spirit of the Lord is upon me. Jesus said, because he anointed me to preach the gospel to the poor. He has sent me to proclaim release to the captive and recovery of sight to the blind, to set free those who are oppressed, to proclaim the favorable year of the Lord."

Through the power of the Gospel, our Kingdom Assignment aids towards the setting free of people who are locked up in their mind, in their heart, in life's choices.

---

3 - Davis, Jim and Graham, Michael. *The Great Dechurching*. (Zondervan: Grand Rapids, MI), 2023.

We are bringing people good news! Our message is one of great hope. Aren't you glad for that?

We don't need to ask many questions about *why* people are hurting to accept the fact that they *are* hurting. This is a privileged season of life we have in order to learn, refine, and implement what God has for us. The fields are indeed white unto harvest. Are you urgently entering the fields each day, surveying the landscape for ways to "bring in the sheaves"?

My Turning Point

I found my own Kingdom Assignment on January 6, 2003, when I came home from work and I found my son, Kevin, unconscious. We rode in the ambulance to the hospital, and a hundred hours later we recognized that his assignment on Earth was over; he went home to be with the Lord. When my 16-year-old son went home to be with the Lord, my life was changed forever. I only thought there was urgency in my life before that event. But believe me, after that traumatic event, even now, more than 20 years later, there is a sense of urgency and a burning within me that I can barely begin to express to you.

Finding your Kingdom Assignment might take you through the valley of the shadow of death. It might raise questions in you you've never had before. It did me.

"What were you thinking, God? Is this the best you can do for me? Do you really expect me to tell people how great you are every single Sunday?"

Through a period of four months of deep, deep grief and discouragement, God spoke to me. He became my Way Maker once again. He became my Miracle Worker once again. He became my Promise Keeper once again. He became my light in the darkness of my soul. Or, I might say, I realized he had never stopped being those things all along.

So I'm not sharing with you a story that belongs to someone else. I'm sharing with you my story, just as you have your own story. As I discovered there was a new normal to be experienced, I discovered there was a new passion in my soul, a new sense of urgency, and the *why* had never been clearer.

There's another part of my story that happened in 2015. It also creates urgency within me. I was invited to go to an Oregon Youth Authority correctional facility called Hillcrest. It was an invitation to visit with some of the kids incarcerated there. As I made my way into that facility and saw the nineteen youths who were in front of me and the staff that were surrounding them, I didn't really know what to say to them. But I found a new sense of urgency.

These are minors. Some of them had not made wise decisions; others, perhaps, got trapped in a system they shouldn't have been in and couldn't now get out of. They need *the* Way Maker. They need *the* Promise Keeper. They need *the* Light in the darkness. What a privilege it is to have this Kingdom Assignment, being able to share with them on a regular basis. God has allowed me to continue doing it since 2015.

I share these stories with you to illustrate my own journey of Transformational Living and to encourage you with everything in me to discover your Kingdom Assignment. Why? Because although my son knew the Lord and loved him dearly and deeply there are 16-year-olds who are dying without Christ. Because there are many teenagers who are behind bars, needing the good news that Jesus loves them, died for them, and is coming back for them if they turn to him.

What Gives You a Sense of Urgency?

Now that I've shared a couple of my stories, what are some of the stories in your own life that give you a sense of urgency? Perhaps it was a bad accident in which you were severely injured, or the untimely death of a classmate in high school, a family member walking away from the faith, or a report you read about human trafficking. Whatever has happened in your life that focuses you on eternity and raises in you an urgency about eternity is what God can use to get you focused on your Kingdom Assignment.

But it isn't only some kind of tragedy that awakens a sense of urgency. The power of God's Word impressed on us through the Holy Spirit is a sure way to make us focus on the needs of those around us and how God wants to use us—to use you!

Ask yourself these questions and write the answers in a journal or the end of this chapter:

- When I'm reading the Word, what am I motivated to do?
- When I'm listening to my pastor preach, what stands out most frequently?
- What do my spiritual mentors say I would have a big impact doing?
- Which "heroes of the faith" challenge me the most? In what ways?
- What would it look like for my spiritual desires, my skills, and my job to align?

Now review those answers and ask God to show you your Kingdom Assignment, because "the night is almost gone, and the day is near" (Romans 13:12). This will be significant when you start developing your Kingdom Business Plan.

Perhaps no story in the Bible better illustrates the nearness of eternity than Jesus' story of the rich man and

Lazarus in Luke 16:19–31. It's a great missionary text as far as I'm concerned because we have two individuals: one rich, one poor. The one who is rich goes to hell and the one who is poor goes to heaven. There's a conversation that goes on with Abraham, the Old Testament saint, and this rich man, who asks, "Can you please send Lazarus (the poor man) back to my family and tell them about this place that I am in? This is a place of torment. It is a place of utter destruction. It is a place that I don't want them to come to. I love them too much for them to have to experience what I am experiencing." It's easy to see this rich man experiencing a sense of urgency. He now knew the why, but it was too late for him.

Every single assignment goes towards someone coming to Christ. Your Kingdom Assignment matters to God and it matters to someone on this earth. There are people that you can reach that I can never reach, and there are people that I can reach that you could never reach. But together we're able to make a difference in this world as we discover and live our own Kingdom Assignment.

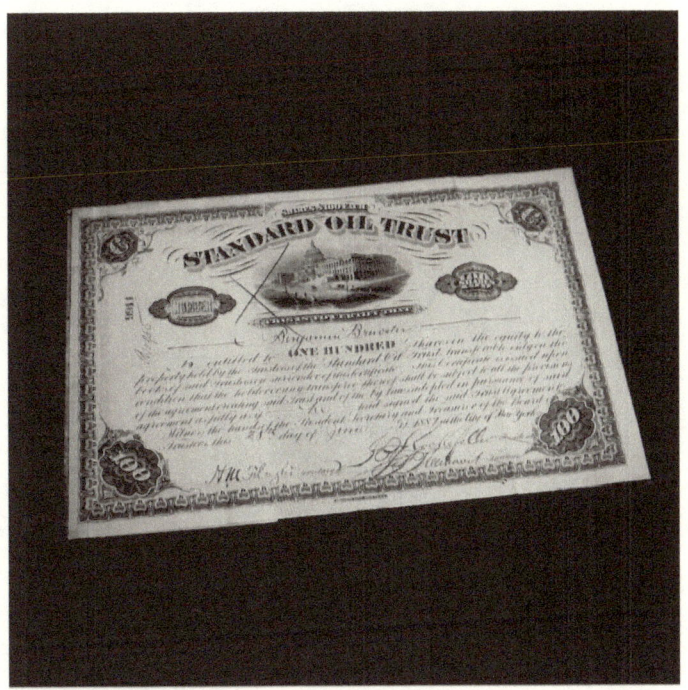

Standard Oil Trust stock certificate dated June 28, 1887, signed by John D. Rockefeller and Henry Flagler.

Chapter Three

LEVERAGE

In his book, *The Great Pierpont Morgan,* Frederick Allen twice recounts a story from the life of J.P. Morgan. It shows how the industrialist used men of character as leverage in his life's work.

> *Over and over he stated this conviction, but never more effectively than in the passage which I have already quoted at the beginning of this book and now quote once more at its end, as Pierpont Morgan's final apologia.*
> *"Is not commercial credit based primarily upon money or property?" asked Untermyer.*

"No, sir," said Morgan; "the first thing is character."

"Before money or property?"

"Before anything else. Money cannot buy it... Because a man I do not trust could not get money from me on all the bonds in Christendom."[4]

Leverage is defined as "the exertion of force by means of a lever or an object used in the manner of a lever" (New Oxford American Dictionary); or "the action of a lever or the mechanical advantage gained by it (Merriam-Webster). In the world of finance, it refers to using borrowed money to finance an investment. It can also refer to using your influence to get results.

Related to my Kingdom Assignment I think of leverage as the multiplication of what I otherwise could not do. Now, how does this work? How can I multiply something that is already beyond my ability? Through the presence and power of the Holy Spirit!

At the end of Luke's gospel, after Jesus's crucifixion and burial, he is alive—resurrected from the dead by the power of God. As he progresses toward the conclusion of his earthly ministry, we read some instructions he gives to his disciples: "And behold, I'm sending the promise of

---

4 - Allen, Frederick Lewis. *The Great Pierpont Morgan*, (Harper & Brothers, New York), 1949, p 282.

my Father upon you, but you are to stay in Jerusalem until you are clothed with power from on high" (Luke 24:49).

What in the world does that mean and what does that look like to be "clothed with power from on high"? I can be clothed with power from on high? You can as well? Can all of God's people be clothed with power from on high?

Yes; each child of God is clothed with power from on high. Conversion not only means receiving salvation in Jesus. It means Jesus sending the Holy Spirit to indwell us. The Holy Spirit is put in us as Comforter, Counselor, Teacher, Guide, Convicter, and put on us as clothing.

Your Kingdom Assignment requires more than your natural talent, your developed skill, or your acquired experience. It requires being clothed with power from on high—the Holy Spirit leading your life from inside out.

Thinking About Leverage

The unique thing about leverage in God's kingdom is it does not matter how much *we* have, but how much *he* has. Earthly leverage depends on means: money, power, or position. Leverage in the Kingdom depends on availability, obedience, and God's will. Think about what James wrote:

Come now, you who say, 'Today or tomorrow we will go to such and such a city, and spend a year there and engage in business and make a profit.' Yet you do not know what your life will be like tomorrow. You are just a vapor that appears for a little while and then vanishes away. Instead, you ought to say, 'If the Lord wills, we will live and also do this or that.' But as it is, you boast in your arrogance; all such boasting is evil. Therefore, to one who knows the right thing to do and does not do it, to him it is sin. (4:13–17)

It isn't our planning that gives us leverage. It isn't our wisdom that gives us leverage. For the one clothed in the Holy Spirit, it is knowing and doing the will of God that provides leverage in fulfilling his or her Kingdom Assignment.

Think about the young boy (the Apostle John calls him a "lad") who among more than 5,000 people was the only one who thought to bring lunch! Jesus took the five barley loaves and two fish, multiplied them and fed the multitude. The lad had no leverage at all. He could not have multiplied his lunch. All he could have done without Jesus was eat it.

But in obedience he gave his lunch to the disciples who brought it to Jesus who performed a miracle. The lad's leverage was his obedience. It wasn't the boy's power, but Jesus' power. The boy did his Kingdom Assignment and Jesus fed a multitude.

Leverage for the people of God isn't what we can do in our strength, it's what he can do in his strength through us. It's what happens when what we hold in our hands is then placed in the hands of Jesus. He then multiplies it and hands it back to us to steward.

Many People can Create Leverage

I'm from the Willamette Valley, in Oregon. I live in the Salem-Keizer area, and it's a beautiful place. There's a highway that goes over Mount Hood. (You can Google it if you want to take a look.)

One day my wife and I were coming back from Central Oregon over Mount Hood on Highway 26. We were in the forested area but not quite to Mount Hood yet. The car ahead of us suddenly stopped and we noticed that a Douglas fir tree had fallen from one side of the road to the other side of the road, blocking the road both directions. Now, Douglas fir trees by nature are very tall and large. This one was not an extremely large tree, but it was large enough that it easily blocked the road.

Here's something that's *usually* true in the state of Oregon: if you have a line of cars and trucks coming over the mountain from central Oregon to the Willamette Valley, there's a fair likelihood that someone's going to have a chainsaw. Maybe even more than one someone. Chainsaws are very common in Oregon since there's a lot of wood to cut. I thought surely there would be someone in this traffic jam who would have a chainsaw, but there was not one to be found!

We were car number two stopped by the tree on our side. I got out, surveyed the situation and looked on the other side of the tree where more cars are starting to pile up. Other people got out and surveyed the situation. People began asking, "What are we going to do?"

One individual suggested we call the state police. I said, "I don't think that's going to work; we'll be here forever by the time they get here. Why don't *we* move the tree?"

Now there were a number of people who thought I was crazy, and maybe I was, but I thought if we get enough people to help we can move that tree off the road.

I began asking people, "Would you be willing to stand shoulder to shoulder and to try and move this Douglas fir off of the highway?"

Since we didn't have a real foreman, I decided to be the foreman that day, encouraging people to line up and down the tree. When I gave the command for our first attempt to move that Douglas fir, nothing happened. We couldn't even budge it. Remember, it was a great big fir tree. So we waited a few minutes for more people to come and more people came until we had filled the length of that entire tree with people shoulder to shoulder. We gave the command, "Move...Move...Move."

Slowly, but surely, inch by inch, we began to move that Douglas fir from across the road to the side of the road. When we were done, there was an applause and celebration that you would not believe. You would've thought we had just watched our favorite team win the Super Bowl.

It truly was incredible, a powerful experience. I will never forget that day when we moved the Douglas fir off the highway to the side of the road without a chainsaw. Without the help of state troopers, a bulldozer, or crane, we were able to move that tree. Why? Because we stood shoulder to shoulder and because we worked as one. That's the power of leverage.

The insight for us here is that leverage isn't simply about what *I* can do for God's kingdom, but what *we* can do. It's like the ingredients for a cake or for a cookie. You need all the ingredients for it to work. You leave one out, you'll know it. Substitute salt for sugar and you'll really know it!

We need to have all the ingredients, and the ingredients are our collective assignments in God's kingdom. Assignments, working together, standing shoulder to shoulder, hearing the command from God, saying, move to the left, move to the right, stand still, move forward, move backwards, shoulder to shoulder, as one. That's leverage.

Unity as a Witness

It's important for us to work together as we live out our Kingdom Assignments because unity is a witness to God's kingdom. We live in a polarized time. People are against each other for all kinds of reasons. Political extremism is higher than ever. People in society need to see God's people in unity!

In Mark 8:11–13, we read, "The Pharisees came out and began to argue with Him, seeking from Him a sign from heaven, to test Him. Sighing deeply in His spirit, He said, 'Why does this generation seek for a sign? Truly I say to you, no sign will be given to this generation.' Leaving them, He again embarked and went away to the other side."

Today as then, people are looking for signs that something is real. Can you blame them? In a divided world unity can be a witness to the work of God. People need to see that we have been touched by Jesus so we can make an eternal difference in their lives. People in this world are looking to see that we love them, that God is real, that Jesus is alive, that his promises are true, and that heaven is available to them through Jesus Christ.

The world's waiting for the body of Christ to stand shoulder to shoulder. I believe that that's what God is wanting to do in his people: gather Kingdom Assignments. Not for individuality, not so that someone can become a superstar, not so that someone can somehow find fame or fortune, but so that we can stand together, God leveraging his power through us, and move mountains for the kingdom of God.

This coin commemorates the first stone laid at the 1907 Hague Conference towards the Peace Palace, completed in 1913. Carnegie donated $1.5 million which is equal to around $50 million adjusted for inflation.

Chapter Four

STEWARDSHIP

||||||||||||||||||||||||

The industrialists had great influence in various spheres of influence. J.P. Morgan, for instance, had tremendous influence in New York City. He had influence around the world, to be sure, but he had great influence through his local church, St. George's Episcopal Church. Morgan wanted to make a difference in his city and he did.

Morgan had the means to make a difference through his wealth. He bought lights for the church building which they had never had before. He arranged for the construction of a basement gymnasium for the youth from the church to enjoy. It was the first of its kind. Talk about being a revolutionary-type thinker! Talk about being a person who believed in the impossible. That was J.P. Morgan.

He built a facility for women and children to experience relief from the summertime heat. He built a home for wayward kids. Working with his pastor, they led many projects to change the city of New York. He understood the power of influence as he stewarded what God had given to him. But it wasn't only his money; it was his testimony.

In addition to the ways he ministered in his local church, J.P. Morgan was in charge of the 1889 tri-annual, national business meeting of the Episcopalian church. He was in charge of the food. He was in charge of the seating. He was in charge of the Book of Common Prayer committee. He was in charge of logistics. He made sure each attendee from all over the country had an assigned seat. All of this was his responsibility.

This great financial mogul of the United States helped people with food and finding seating and housing. It was a three-week-long convention. Morgan did it not because he was asked to do it, but because he felt compelled to do it. It was a part of his Kingdom Assignment.

Taken together, we can see Morgan's stewardship in five areas: influence, time, talent, testimony, and treasure.

Think about it this way: what we are thinking and believing we can connect to the head and the heart. With your head think about what you do with your time, then with your heart think about how you use the talents and spend the treasure God has given you. Taken together these things become your testimony of how God transforms your life for his kingdom purpose.

Influence

We have influence without even realizing it. There are people watching us and listening to us. For those reasons alone our Kingdom Assignment means a great deal. There are people for whom we can make a difference in their lives. When we underestimate the power of influence, we miss what God can do through us to touch others.

One prominent parable Jesus taught about the kingdom of God is found in Luke 14:16–24.

> But he said to him, 'A man once gave a great banquet and invited many. And at the time for the banquet he sent his servant to say to those who had been invited, "Come, for everything is now ready." But they all alike began to make excuses. The first said to him, "I have bought a field, and I must go out and see it. Please have me excused." And another said, "I have bought five yoke of oxen, and I go to examine them. Please

have me excused." And another said, "I have married a wife, and therefore I cannot come." So the servant came and reported these things to his master. Then the master of the house became angry and said to his servant, "Go out quickly to the streets and lanes of the city, and bring in the poor and crippled and blind and lame." And the servant said, "Sir, what you commanded has been done, and still there is room." And the master said to the servant, "Go out to the highways and hedges and compel people to come in, that my house may be filled. For I tell you, none of those men who were invited shall taste my banquet."' (ESV)

Focus on how influence is used in this parable: the man sent his servant to bring those he had invited to the dinner. When each of them made excuses, the servant went to those who lacked any kind of station, wherever they were, and *compelled* them to come to the dinner.

It's easy to see the urgency here as well. The man hosting the dinner—representative of God—expects his servants to do as they are instructed, using all their influence and every means of leverage they have to compel people into his kingdom. Going into the hedges and the byways, compelling people to come to Jesus requires a reprioritization of our spiritual lives.

It's a reprioritization of our time, talent, treasure, and influence to fit a Kingdom Assignment.

You might see now how your testimony is a result of Transformational Living that affects every aspect of your life. Your head, your heart, your hands together stewarding your treasure and influence sharing the gospel with others. Those who are involved in business share it through business thinking and dealings. Those who are involved in the arts share it through their art. Those who are involved in industry share it through industry. Those who are in education, share it through academic and intellectual means. But, by all means, we are used by God together.

In 1 Corinthians 12, the Bible speaks about spiritual gifts. Every believer has a spiritual gift. It is important for us to understand God gives us spiritual gifts to multiply our Kingdom impact. Not only do we have a Kingdom Assignment, but we have a spiritual gift that empowers us to accomplish it. Notice in verses 4–7: "Now there are varieties of gifts, but the same Spirit. And there are varieties of ministries, and the same Lord. There are varieties of effects, but the same God who works all things in all *persons*. But to each one is given the manifestation of the Spirit for the common good."

In addition to 1 Corinthians 12, Paul lists spiritual gifts in Romans 12:4–8, then in 1 Peter 4:7–11, we read:

The end of all things is near; therefore, be of sound judgment and sober spirit for the purpose of prayer. Above all, keep fervent in your love for one another, because love covers a multitude of sins. Be hospitable to one another without complaint. As each one has received a special gift, employ it in serving one another as good stewards of the manifold grace of God. Whoever speaks, is to do so as one who is speaking the utterances of God; whoever serves is to do so as one who is serving by the strength which God supplies; so that in all things God may be glorified through Jesus Christ, to whom belongs the glory and dominion forever and ever. Amen.

It's easy to see how some Christians really are gung-ho about spiritual gifts! God gifts us and expects us to use the gifts for his glory. The influence we have when the Holy Spirit uses the gift or gifts in us can be mighty!

But there is a warning. Gifts can become a source of pride, drawing attention to us instead of God. That's why Paul reminds us in 1 Corinthians 13 that all the spiritual gifts in the world are useless without love. When our Kingdom Assignment is energized by our spiritual gift we can experience a tremendous move of the Spirit, and if it is truly from the Spirit it will be bathed in love.

Love must permeate our assignment, including our spiritual gifts, throughout our life. People need to see the love of Christ through us. Our Kingdom Assignment should bring us to a place of humility. Knowing that Jesus loved us helps us love others. "We love," John tells us, "because he first loved us" (1 John 4:19).

Fleshing it Out

What I'm doing here is fleshing out our Kingdom Assignment, trying to show how it works with each person. Our Kingdom Assignment is specific to our spiritual giftings, our experience, and our call from God. Each person's Kingdom Assignment will look different; that's not only okay, it's by God's design.

I pastored a church for a number of years. During my time there, we had multiple building programs. As we were going through one of these programs, we came up against a wall in which we were running short of funds. We were in desperate need of more money to continue the project. As a result, in order to save a few dollars, a few people were doing extra things around the facility. One of my "extra" responsibilities was to clean up the sanctuary before Sunday.

One day as I was cleaning, I noticed that there was a piece of paper on the altar. It was an envelope. I threw it in the waste basket along with the other pieces of paper that were strewn throughout. There was a little of everything, from people writing on their bulletins to people writing on the giving envelope cards to most any scrap of paper.

A candy wrapper? It's amazing what happens during a sermon.

As I was throwing away the garbage, quite literally the Lord spoke to me and said, "You threw something away you shouldn't have thrown away." Now the Lord had spoken to me many times in that particular place; he's been very close to me. I thought, this is an odd thing for the Lord to say to me. He said, "Go back to the garbage can." I went back to the garbage can. He said, "Pull out that envelope. I want you to open up the envelope." I opened the envelope and in it was a cashier's check for the exact amount of money that was needed in order for us to continue the project! I won't say how much money it was, but it was a large enough sum of money that you wouldn't dare have thrown that much away. At least that's how I define a six-figure check!

Part of our Kingdom Assignment is recognizing there is no garbage in God's kingdom; everything and everyone has value to him. I hope that resonates with you. We are to be proactive with all people groups in all places at all times as best we can. We don't always get it right. Sometimes the pastor throws a large check away in a garbage can! But we do our best to keep a Kingdom focus at all times. To this end, we steward what God has given us, which leads to effective influence.

Wherever God places you and me with our Kingdom Assignments, we are to compel people through our testimony to come into the fold, to come into the presence of God, to invite Jesus into life and into our hearts as Lord and Savior, and to experience the presence of God in a profound way. You know, there are many people who are not experiencing the peace of God, yet the Bible says in Philippians 4:6–7, "Be anxious for nothing but in everything by prayer and supplication, with thanksgiving, let your request be made known unto God. And the peace of God, which goes beyond human understanding, will guard your hearts and minds in Christ Jesus."

We live in a time that many people are anxious. Bad news consumes them and their hearts and minds are in constant upheaval. As a result, our communities, our nation, and our world lack peace. As we live our Kingdom Assignment we will bring the peace of God, this peace of Jesus Christ, to people. Remember he says in John chapter 20, "My peace I give unto you, my peace I leave with you."

Influence on You and Your Influence on Others

Before I close this chapter, I want you to think about the person in your life who had the most positive influence on you. Perhaps a parent, a teacher, a pastor, a friend, a mentor, a boss, or even a sibling. Why did you listen to her or him? What made you want to put into practice things they taught or showed you?

It's very likely you knew they really loved you. You also realized at some point they really wanted to help you. No doubt as you watched their life or work you saw something that impacted you enough to want it in your own life. For most of us, the person who had the most positive influence took time, was intentional, was patient, and, often, loved us deeply.

If a person like that influenced you, that's what it will take for you to influence others. Your Kingdom Assignment, energized by your spiritual gift, will see its maximum impact when you use your influence in the lives of others in the same way you were influenced.

As we all steward our Kingdom Assignment locally, we will see global impact for the kingdom of God!

This piece of steel is a cut from the first steel coming from the Bessemer blast furnace on August 26, 1875, at 5:45pm.

Chapter Five

TIME AND HEAD

John D. Rockefeller was in church every single Sunday. He took the Sabbath day for rest. Here's a businessman who built the largest industry of his time, Standard Oil, yet he took one out of seven days to rest. One out of seven days to be with God. One out of seven days to be with his family in prayer. One out of seven days to be in church, to teach, to study, to learn.

We have something to learn from the Industrialists. They were the biggest and the best in their industries in their time of American history. Understanding how they lived will help us live the way we ought to before God. They might just help us understand as well that living our

Kingdom Assignment isn't about adding something else to our crowded schedule. Instead, it's about a transformed way of living that makes our Kingdom Assignment the regular flow of our lives.

Many people—you might be one of them—use some kind of "time management system" to help them be more efficient. Whether you use a system or not, we need to constantly remember our need to take seriously our time on this earth. Christians have eternal life, but our days here are numbered. In the words of the Psalmist, our days are "just inches long" (39:5).

How will you spend your time? Because that is how you will spend your days and your life.

What Matters Most

For part of my Kingdom Assignment, several years ago, God opened the door for me to spend time at the Oregon Youth Authority and I continue to do so to this day. I'm a volunteer, usually going once a week. If I'm having a bad day, I go to the youth facility. If I want to be encouraged, I go to the youth facility. If I want to be uplifted, I go to the youth facility and I put myself in the circle of those youth.

Between 2016–2019, I was privileged to baptize 272 of the youth held there. One day I was baptizing seven of these young people. During baptism there are no spectators; none of the other youth are allowed to watch. They keep them separated for safety and security reasons, but for some reason, this one youth was allowed to come and watch the others get baptized. I didn't know why. It certainly wasn't the normal policy. But for whatever reason he was there, and it was fine by me.

I baptized these youth, one after the other, one through seven. When number seven came up out of the water, there was applause from the other young people and staff as there was for the previous six. As he got out of the water and up the steps, a towel was handed to him. As he began drying himself, the boy who was observing stood up, came over rapidly, and jumped right in the pool. Well, that put the staff at a little bit more alert! He came towards me, stood in front of me and said, "Right here, right now."

I said, "What?"

He said, "I want Jesus in my heart right now and I want to be baptized, too." I led that young man to Christ in the water, and upon him receiving Christ, I baptized him.

It was like reenacting Phillip and the Ethiopian eunuch from Acts 8 in an Oregon youth facility baptizing pool! What a joy!

Whether at a youth facility, a job location, your local church, a homeless shelter, a food bank, or an international mission trip, the question for all of us is: how will we spend the time the Lord has given us? The reason for identifying your Kingdom Assignment and giving your time, talent, treasure, and influence is because all of us have limited time on earth!

Here's what scripture says in Ephesians 5:15–16: "Therefore be careful how you walk, not as unwise men but as wise, making the most of your time, because the days are evil."

Do you ever think about how you spend your time? Do you realize how quickly life passes? Anyone you ever meet who is in their 70s or 80s will tell you the same thing: just yesterday I was a teenager. "Time waits for no man" is more than a motivational slogan. It's the reality of being on this earth. The seconds tick away, the hours pass, the days come and go, the calendar pages are torn away, and nothing ever slows them down.

It's because time marches on that we must make every moment count. Our Kingdom Assignment depends on us understanding how to steward our time. In Ecclesiastes 9:10 we read, "Whatever your hand finds to do, do *it* with *all* your might; for there is no activity or planning or knowledge or wisdom in Sheol [the grave] where you are going." In other words, do what you can now; you can't do anything after you die. Then the words of Jesus, "We must work the works of Him who sent Me as long as it is day; night is coming when no one can work" (John 9:4).

No one knows when they won't be able to do anything for the Lord. We can't foresee a debilitating illness, a severe car-wreck followed by multiple surgeries, or some other cause of inability to serve as we once did. Further, we don't know when our Kingdom Assignment will end, so we want to be all in with God from the very beginning.

Now is the time to do our best and give our best to the work of the Lord. Every person counts; every person matters to Jesus. We are finite and human and can only do so much in a given day. And because we are finite, we must make the most of our time the best way that we know.

Using our Time

The Bible indicates the times near Christ's return will be like they were in the days of Noah. Well, what was going on in the days of Noah? They were busy; they were preoccupied; they ignored God. Life was happening. Is it any different today? No. Life is happening. Life is busy, life is full. We have very limited time.So it's important for us to figure out how to manage our time, determine what matters most, and not leave out our Kingdom Assignment, making sure that it's an important part of all that we do every single day.

One of the reasons for taking this journey together is so we can encourage one another to stay involved in our Kingdom Assignment and not have a lapse of time. This is why we encourage this journey with friends, family, church family, or coworkers. We encourage people to take this journey together so that we don't lose heart and give up and quit and say that I'm no longer going to participate.

What if every Christian discovered their Kingdom Assignment and determined to help at least one person every day? I gave myself the same challenge I gave to the congregation I served for many years: each one reach one. For us to help at least one person every day over the course of a year means 365 people are touched. That is profound and prophetic; it is life giving and life changing. Let me encourage you to ask yourself daily: How can I multiply my influence today? Not twenty years from now, but today. This day.

Transformational Living is about heart change that leads to life change. None of us want to come to an end of a day and say, "I sure wasted this day." No, we want to make the most of each day. We want good things to happen in our day. We want things to happen that are eternal, that make a difference in people's lives, things that count, that count for eternity. Now is the time. Now is the day of salvation.

The Bible makes God's invitation clear. The most well-known verse in all of scripture is John 3:16, "For God so loved the world, that He gave His only begotten Son, that whoever believes in Him shall not perish, but have eternal life." The last book of the Bible, the Revelation, contains some of the most beautiful, the most precious words in all of scripture: "The Spirit and the bride say, 'Come.' And let the one who hears say, 'Come.' And let the one who is thirsty come; let the one who wishes take the water of life without cost" (22:17).

Upon selling Carnegie Steel to U.S. Steel effective March 1, 1901, Carnegie's first order of business was to fund libraries in New York City. His gift of $5.2 million led to the first 65 Carnegie Libraries.

Chapter Six

TALENT AND HANDS

IIIIIIIIIIIIIIIIIII

Everyone has talent, a natural aptitude or ability. For many people, a particular talent is revealed early. A young child displays advanced hand-eye coordination and excels in baseball, softball, or tennis. Another displays an "ear for music" and goes beyond other kids in piano or guitar.

Other people don't seem to have a particular talent as a child but find it after they are grown. A woman finds, in the second half of life, a talent for writing novels or a man discovers the ability to run long distances with less training than other guys his age.

Whether or not your talent is physical or mental, everyone has talent that can be used in their Kingdom Assignment. Christians should think about talent less as a natural ability and more as a God-given ability. It's something God has gifted you to do that isn't necessarily a spiritual gift.

I would be one who would say I'm not very good at a lot of things. I'm not one who can change my oil in my car. I tried it—once. I won't do it again! It was a miserable experience.

But some of you can do it with your eyes closed. I can't put anything together without using the instructions. Some people have an engineering mind and don't have to look at the instructions at all. They can see the finished product in their head.

The uniqueness of these talents and the combination of Kingdom Assignments means God can use all of us together to change the world. Our talents aren't just for enjoyment or trophies; they are ways God uses us for his glory.

In the Old Testament we read of the building of the tabernacle, its sides and top, and the furniture and implements the priests would use. In Exodus 25–30 we read the incredible detail given by God for how everything was to be made. Then, in chapter 31, God assigned the craftsmen Bezalel, Oholiab, and "all who are skillful" the tasks of constructing everything. God gave them talents then called on them to use those talents.

God was clear about this. He says, "I have called" and "I Myself have appointed" (vs 2, 6). It was no accident that skilled workers were chosen then, and God is looking to use our skills today.

I've chosen hands to connect with talent because so many times hands express our talent. Whether painting, carving, building, writing, throwing, or any other ability, our hands often help us express it. So when you think of *hands*, think of *talent*.

Divine Intervention

Every God-given talent is for the purpose of equipping for a God-given assignment. God doesn't waste his gifts and we shouldn't either. Everything God does is for a purpose, down to whether we do math well, speak in public well, paint portraits well, or have a great understanding of business principles. It is God who is at work through us.

When I say "divine intervention," I'm really talking about the miraculous way God works in us. Not every miracle is the parting of the Red Sea, but all miracles are divine intervention. It isn't our talent alone that accomplishes the work of God; it's God working in us, intervening in our lives to do his will.

David was good with a slingshot before he faced Goliath. His talent was honed, and he was a skilled hunter. He had already killed lions and bears who threatened his father's flocks (1 Samuel 17:34–37). Yet even King Saul, who was too scared to fight the giant, recognized David would need God's help, telling him, "Go, and may the Lord be with you" (v 38).

Samson's talent was innate and God-given. His strength was unmatched no matter who he fought. When, as a young man, he was attacked by a lion he killed it with his bare hands (Judges 14:5, 6). Scripture records specifically that "the Spirit of the Lord came powerfully on him." In a single battle, armed only with the jawbone of a dead donkey, he killed a thousand men (15:15–17). In another instance he pulled up doors and gateposts in Gaza and carried them several miles to Hebron (16:3).

Another well-known incident in Samson's life took place at his tragic death. Blinded, bound, and the object of mockery, he asked God for strength just once more. Empowered by God, Samson collapsed the pillars of a Philistine temple, causing the deaths of those mocking him (Judges 16:26–30).

Samson is a good lesson about how talent isn't enough. Regardless of his super-human strength, when Samson's heart grew cold toward God, he could no longer depend on his might. His pride was his downfall, and it can be ours as well.

Even Jesus, whose teachings were so powerful it was said of him, "never did anyone speak like this," relied on the power of the Holy Spirit—divine intervention—to complete his Kingdom Assignment.

If the talents of these Bible heroes (and others) as well as our Savior depend on divine intervention, how much more should we depend on the Spirit to multiply the ministry of our hands?

Talent in the Life of Rockefeller

In her book, *John D. Rockefeller: The Cleveland Years*, Grace Goulder writes of the oil industrialist, "He was no novice in the role of chairman, for he had learned the art as a teen-ager when appointed head of the Erie Street Church's board of trustees, all older than he. Except for Colonel Payne, the Standard's new directors were also his seniors."[5]

Rockefeller had an unusual talent that Goulder calls an "art": he led and managed people far older than he was. In my denomination, to serve on the Board of Trustees at the local church where I served for 35 years a person had to be at least 21 years of age. I am so glad young Rockefeller did not attend the church I pastored! I would go down in history as the pastor who failed to

5 - Goulder, p 115.

63

utilize the special talents of a young Rockefeller because of a denominational rule.

I became a licensed minister in my denomination at the age of 20, something that few, if any, had accomplished in my generation. To think that young Rockefeller was younger than I was as a leader in his church is quite impressive. To be certain, his talent was sent from heaven above. Once again, evidence that his faith led the way for his future in business.

Talent and Hands Reflect God's Image

Most of you reading these words know that God made the heavens and the earth. Remember how Moses describes it?

> *In the beginning God created the heavens and the earth. Now the earth was formless and empty, darkness covered the surface of the watery depths, and the Spirit of God was hovering over the surface of the waters. Then God said, "Let there be light," and there was light. God saw that the light was good, and God separated the light from the darkness. God called the light "day," and the darkness he called "night." There was an evening, and there was a morning: one day.*
> *Then God said, "Let there be an expanse between the waters, separating water from*

water." So God made the expanse and separated the water under the expanse from the water above the expanse. And it was so. God called the expanse "sky." Evening came and then morning: the second day. (Genesis 1:1–8)

Several more times in this chapter we read of God creating. God could have easily spoken everything into existence at one time, in one word. But he chose not to. He chose to take six days.

When it came to humanity, God didn't even create man and woman at the same time. God made man (Adam) from dust and then made woman (Eve) from Adam.

Then God said, "Let us make man in our image, after our likeness. And let them have dominion over the fish of the sea and over the birds of the heavens and over the livestock and over all the earth and over every creeping thing that creeps on the earth."

So God created man in his own image, in the image of God he created him; male and female he created them. (Genesis 1:27, 28, ESV)

So the Lord God caused a deep sleep to fall upon the man, and while he slept took one of his ribs and closed up its place with flesh. And the rib that the Lord God had taken from the man he

*made into a woman and brought her to the man.
Then the man said,*
  *"This at last is bone of my bones and flesh of
  my flesh; she shall be called Woman,
  because she was taken out of Man."
  (Genesis 2:21–23, ESV)*

The entire creation story shows the creative power of God.

Should it surprise us, then, that God created humans to be creative? That the talent to create comes from the Creator? A part of human flourishing is God giving us the ability to create and to make things with our hands. People flourish when they use their talents for God's glory.

Think about the creativity the five industrialists employed in building their business or industry: Ford's development of the assembly line; Vanderbilt's timing in moving from ferry boats, to steamships, to railroads; Carnegie's vision for steel in construction; Rockefeller's expansion of Standard Oil into a conglomerate; Morgan's bailout of the banking system was but one of his creative moves, with financing Thomas Edison's drive to electrify the country and the railroad system being two others.

Opening the Door for Your Talent

A warning is appropriate here: simply because you have talent, even great talent, doesn't mean people will be interested in what you can do. If you have a scowl or a bad attitude, few people will care how well you can play guitar or build a spreadsheet.

I have noticed several ways that people behave that are attractive. Let's look at three of them: a smiling face, a listening ear, and a kind demeanor.

Are we attracted to kindness? I am. I'm attracted to kind people. I'm attracted to people who smile. I don't smile as much as I wished I could smile! There are some people who naturally just smile all the time.

Have we ever sat with someone and just listened to them spill out their concerns, burdens, or worries? And when you were done, they would say, "Thanks for helping me. I just can't believe how much this helped me." This has happened to me. It leaves me thinking, "But, I didn't say anything." Sometimes speaking isn't even needed, because listening can speak volumes. Sometimes listening is the answer they've been looking for. They've just been looking for someone who cares enough to listen. Being a good listener opens the door for you to exercise your Kingdom Assignment.

Not only that, but listening is a way we express love. Listening is love and love is listening. Jesus speaks about this very thing in John 15:12–15:

"My command is this: Love each other as I have loved you. Greater love has no one than this: to lay down one's life for one's friends. You are my friends if you do what I command. I no longer call you servants, because a servant does not know his master's business. Instead, I have called you friends, for everything that I learned from my Father I have made known to you." (NIV)

But what a difference the body of Christ could make if we would just smile, listen, and be kind! Whatever our Kingdom Assignment, and however God activates our talents to complete it, we have to smile, listen, and be kind.

We are his hands. We are his feet. We are his smile extended. I would say to a congregation, if we would just be kind, we'd grow by 10%. If we would just smile, we would grow by another 10%.

It's an amazing thing what happens when people smile, when they are kind, and when they listen. Of all the people in the world who should be marked by these, it's God's people. Just imagine how your Kingdom Assignment will be fulfilled when you open doors with these three traits.

In 1867, Cornelius Vanderbilt took ownership of this New York Central Rail Road, adding to it the Hudson River Rail Road in 1869. This July 24,1874 ticket stub was for a ride on the "N. Y. Central and Hudson River R. R."

Chapter Seven

TESTIMONY AND HEART

||||||||||||||||||||||||

Most everyone today is familiar with the idea of a *testimonial*. It's a written or verbal affirmation to the excellent work or trustworthiness of someone else. You'll find them on websites, ads, books, and billboards. If you want to promote your business, it helps to have others recommend you. Their recommendations come in the form of testimonials.

A *testimony* is similar, but it's what you tell about something you know personally. A witness in court gives testimony to what he or she personally witnessed. The jury weighs the witnesses' testimonies for truthfulness before giving a verdict.

My favorite show growing up and even to this day is Perry Mason. It was on at noon on channel 12 in Portland until cable came along. Even then I think it was still on channel 12. I never knew who did it until at the very end of the show and even though I had seen the episodes over and over, they were written so well I could not remember who was guilty until the last few minutes of the show. I loved the court part where the witnesses were asked questions and gave testimony to what they had seen or heard.

When we tell others what God is doing in our lives, we are giving a testimony. Our testimony of what God has done forms a basis for our Kingdom Assignment. When we talk about Transformational Living, it's the pinnacle of your time, talents, treasure, and influence through the power of the Holy Spirit working in us. Every Christian has a testimony. Every Christian's testimony is a miracle. Your testimony tells of your experience with Jesus and shows how your time with Jesus can make a difference in the lives of people around you. It's a heart-story of God at work in you.

Mary Magdalene had a tremendous testimony. Not only had Jesus delivered her from demonic possession, she was one of the women who saw Jesus alive after his resurrection—even before the eleven apostles! Matthew writes in his gospel:

> *Now after the Sabbath, as it began to dawn toward the first day of the week, Mary Magdalene and the other Mary came to look at the grave. And behold, a severe earthquake had occurred, for an angel of the Lord descended from heaven and came and rolled away the stone and sat upon it. And his appearance was like lightning, and his clothing as white as snow. The guards shook for fear of him and became like dead men. The angel said to the women, "Do not be afraid; for I know that you are looking for Jesus who has been crucified. He is not here, for He has risen, just as He said. Come, see the place where He was lying. Go quickly and tell His disciples that He has risen from the dead; and behold, He is going ahead of you into Galilee, there you will see Him; behold, I have told you." (28:1-7)*

Mark's gospel tells us, "She went and reported [that Jesus had risen] to those who had been with Him, while they were mourning and weeping" (16:10). What a testimony Mary had! And here's the thing: even though they didn't believe her (verse 11), she continued to proclaim that Jesus had risen. The other disciples' unbelief didn't make her testimony false!

Don't worry about the people who don't believe your testimony of God's Kingdom Assignment in your life. Many people will and God will use you to impact their lives.

Peter and John were two of those called by Jesus early in his ministry. They also saw Jesus after his resurrection and in John 21 we read about one of those instances. They were fishing when Jesus called them to shore for a meal. I would imagine, for the most part, things were incredibly wonderful. But there's this conversation in which somehow the disciples understood (or misunderstood) that John the beloved was going to get a blessing that none of the other disciples would get. It seemed he would just ascend and be with Jesus and he wouldn't go through pain and suffering and death. Peter was troubled by this and said something to Jesus.

Jesus' response was, "What is that to you? You follow me!" (John 21:22). Jesus made it clear to Peter that whatever did or didn't happen to John was really none of Peter's concern. Peter had his own call to follow Jesus.

The testimony of everyone who accepts their Kingdom Assignment will be different. Some people will make and give a lot of money; some people won't. Some people will personally lead many people to Christ; others, only a few. Some people will have influence with successful businessmen and women; some will never rub shoulders with the well-to-do.

But all of us have our assignment, our place in God's kingdom activity. The writer of Hebrews said that we should "run with endurance the race that is set before us" (12:1). We all have a race, but not all have the same race. Some are running, some are walking, some are driving, and some are flying. I can't run the race set before me if I'm longing to run someone else's race! My Kingdom Assignment keeps me focused on my own race.

Now here's a time for us to take some inventory on the people that bother us, the circumstances that bother us, and the things that aren't right in life. We can lose a lot of joy. We can lose a lot of sleep. We can lose a lot of happiness. We lose if we spend our time looking at what others have and what we don't have. We can spend a lot of time focusing on other people's lives and situations for which we don't really know the whole story. And we can miss out on what our story could be and to be able to say to others in a humble way, "Praise God! I have a Kingdom Assignment."

And I pray that, that if there's anyone or any circumstance troubling you, you would take to heart Jesus' words to Peter, "What is that to you?" Don't let it bother you. God has a Kingdom Assignment for you. Don't be bothered or distracted by others. Don't be bothered by or jealous of what others are accomplishing. Remember, the enemy wants to steal away the joy of knowing God by causing us to think we have absolutely nothing to offer when in fact we know that God has given to us a Kingdom Assignment.

A Kingdom Business Plan

I have a Kingdom Business Plan. It's a plan by which I serve the King of Kings and Lord of Lords. It reminds me how God has blessed me rather than comparing myself to others. Now the Bible is abundantly clear about this. It's one of the reasons God included coveting in the Ten Commandments. Remember the final commandment? "You shall not covet your neighbor's house; you shall not covet your neighbor's wife or his male servant or his female servant or his ox or his donkey or anything that belongs to your neighbor" (Exodus 20:17). To covet is to express dissatisfaction with God by thinking that somehow we're being robbed of a blessing. We haven't been robbed! No, we have been saved. We have been called. We have been given a Kingdom Assignment.

A Kingdom Business Plan is a tool to help Christians discover, develop, devote, discern, and deploy their Kingdom Assignment until it becomes so natural and so normal that it is common. It puts the fine touches on the broad strokes, so you can know the full picture of your Kingdom Assignment. (See the last page of the book for more information on developing your Kingdom Business Plan.)

What if thousands of Christians discovered their purpose? What if they obeyed God sending them where he wants them to be, doing what he wants them to do? What if their head, heart, hands, and influence were aligned with their Kingdom Assignment? Then we could begin to see a move of God from this generation to the next generation and see God do something very special as he has done at other times in our history. I want to see him moving through businesspeople all around the world; men and women who understand their Kingdom Assignment, whose lives reflect being used by the Holy Spirit.

Wouldn't that be something for God to use these five industrialists whom many authors, writers, and journalists have despised and scorned saying that they were the robber-barons and the evil men of their day? When in fact they had a testimony and a Kingdom Assignment! They figured out a way not to be distracted by commentary of those who didn't like them or didn't agree with them, because they had their gaze fixed on Jesus. You might wonder how they did it.

I believe and I would suggest to you that their testimonies drove their business. Their testimonies drove how they approached life. Their relationship with God is what made the difference. They handled the blessings from God understanding that they were stewards.

Preparing and Presenting Your Testimony

If you are a follower of Jesus, you already have what many people call a "salvation testimony." It's what you would share with someone who asks how you came to know Jesus. Many people organize their salvation testimony around three main points:

- My life before Christ
- How I came to know Christ
- My life after Christ

This structure allows you to hit the main points of the gospel using your personal story rather than preaching a sermon. Our separation from God because of sin is expressed in *your life before Christ*. The need for repentance and faith in Jesus alone and the circumstances God lovingly used to bring you to salvation are *how you came to know Christ*. Finally, the ways your life has changed (love for God's word, prayer, desire to see others come to Christ) since Jesus saved you is *your life after Christ*.

Once a person writes their testimony using these three points, they can usually share it in 2–3 minutes. It's like an elevator pitch: being prepared to tell your story in the amount of time it takes to ride an elevator a few floors. This kind of testimony has opened millions of doors for complete gospel presentations, and God will do the same for you. I suggest spending not more than 30 seconds on your life before knowing Jesus, about 30 seconds on how you came to know Christ, then a full two minutes of your life since knowing Jesus. I use this pattern because Jesus is a right now God, a right now Savior, and a right now friend!

Now, think about a Kingdom Assignment. As you begin to experience Transformational Living, and God shows your Kingdom Assignment to you, the third part of your testimony—My life after Christ—will include elements of that Assignment. In other words, God working in you through your Kingdom Assignment will always be a part of your testimony!

After preparing your testimony, you should always be ready to present it. Any time God allows us to talk about him we should. He's always worth giving glory! In Acts 4, Peter and John are arrested for preaching Jesus' resurrection from the dead. When threatened by the religious leaders, the two Apostles appealed to their testimony:

> *And when they had summoned them, they commanded them not to speak or teach at all in the name of Jesus. But Peter and John answered and said to them, 'Whether it is right in the sight of God to give heed to you rather than to God, you be the judge; for we cannot stop speaking about what we have seen and heard.' (vs 18–20)*

We cannot stop speaking about what we have seen and heard. That's the inner drive a testimony gives us; we must talk about Jesus! Your testimony becomes alive when you share in the cross and the empty tomb. Our testimony contains power when we spend time with Christ! From that, we're able to say our mission is to be with Jesus. Our message is one of great hope.

1 Peter 3:15 is another favorite verse of mine. It reads, "But sanctify Christ as Lord in your hearts, always *being* ready to make a defense to everyone who asks you to give an account for the hope that is in you, yet with gentleness and reverence." Again, being ready leads to hope!

I want to encourage you to consider the power of your testimony for Jesus, and the power of a testimony that tells the story of accepting your Kingdom Assignment. Personal stories have impact. Testimonies can't be refuted; it's the story of what God has done and is doing in your life. As we saw with Mary Magdalene, when it's truth, no one can prove it false.

Your testimony will impact people; it will change some people's lives. People who are doubting will be encouraged. People who are weak will be strengthened. People who are confused can receive clarity. And God can do this through you!

Begin to pray about your testimony. If you already have your salvation testimony prepared, pray for opportunities to share it. As you work on your Kingdom Assignment, ask God to give you the words that will help you express what he is doing in your life.

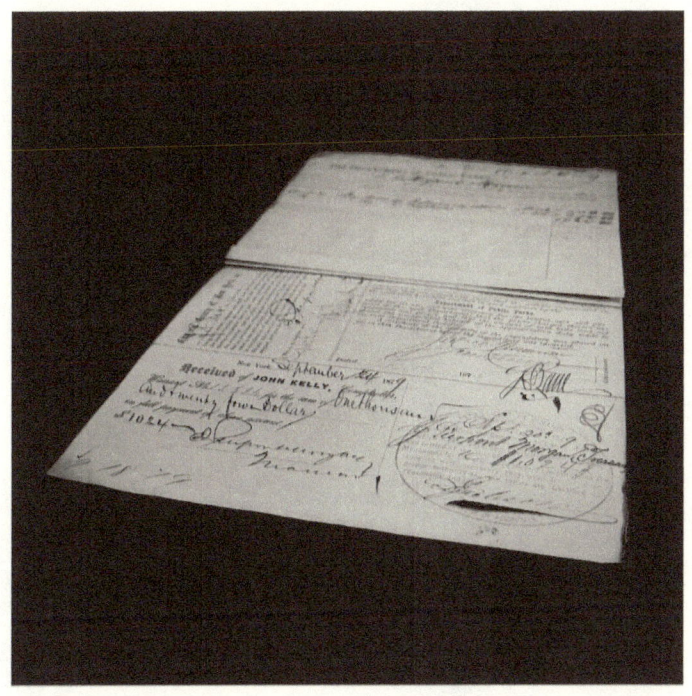

This receipt for donation was signed by J. P. Morgan, a trustee of the American Museum of Natural History for 44 years from 1869 until his death in 1913.

Chapter Eight

TREASURE AND HHH

Up to this point we have been looking at how Transformational Living leads us to our Kingdom Assignment. We've looked at how our head relates to time, our hands relate to talent, and our hearts relate to our testimony.

In this chapter I want to look at how God brings all these together so that we use our treasure for his kingdom.

When we have invested our time and our talent, and we have made our testimony the pinnacle, one of the things that just naturally follows is that our treasure will be deployed as well. We don't begin with treasure.

We conclude that, as a product follows as the intended consequence of its manufacturing, that stewarding our treasure follows our time, talent, and testimony as the intended consequence. When we experience Transformational Living, we have a Kingdom view of our possessions.

Stewardship and Ownership

It's hard not to think about money, isn't it? Most of us think about it every day of our lives. Sometimes we worry about how little we have. How can I make this last until my next payday? What if I run out? Some people get prideful about how much they have and forget it all belongs to God. Rather than looking for ways for their money to help the poor, send missionaries, or support ministries, they buy new cars, boats, or more expensive houses.

What we need to do is think about how God intends for us to use our earthly goods for his kingdom and glory. When we are generous, we will be a blessing to others and to God as well.

You've heard that people follow vision. I would say to you that our treasure follows our testimony. Treasure follows our Kingdom Assignment. Treasure follows our call from God. Treasure follows our time with Jesus. It doesn't lead. It follows.

In 1 Timothy 6:17–20, Paul writes,

Instruct those who are rich in this present world not to be conceited or to fix their hope on the uncertainty of riches, but on God, who richly supplies us with all things to enjoy. Instruct them to do good, to be rich in good works, to be generous and ready to share, storing up for themselves the treasure of a good foundation for the future, so that they may take hold of that which is life indeed.

This passage is straightforward. It speaks about how we should view money in light of God's kingdom. If we focus on verse 19, we can see that the wealthy can "store up for themselves the treasure of a good foundation for the future." Andrew Carnegie believed this. He served God with his wealth in his time and place and God expects us to serve him with our money in our time and place. When asked whether the millions he gave away caused him anxious moments, Carnegie said, "Not a single one, because I am a steward of what God blessed me with."[6] A Carnegie biographer wrote about his peace of mind and his vast wealth, saying, "While millions are

---

6 - Alderson, Barnard. *Andrew Carnegie: The Man and His Work*. (Doubleday, Page & Co.: New York), 1902, p 141.

a burden to some men, and crush both soul and energy, he finds in them no source of anxiety. They are his, and yet they are not. Their disbursement will give him the greatest happiness and abolish all thoughts of anxiety from his mind."[7]

Being a steward is different from being an owner. Stewards know they are responsible for what belongs to another person. The term we're more familiar with today is *manager*. All of us are managers of some amount of "stuff" God allows into our control. Whether an automobile, furniture, clothes, a house, money in the bank or investments, and on and on, God places it under our control to manage.

This is where we often make a mistake: We forget we are stewards/managers and think we are owners. As a result, we view our stuff not as something owned by God, but as treasure that we own. This is why Jesus warned, "Do not store up for yourselves treasures on earth, where moth and rust destroy, and where thieves break in and steal. But store up for yourselves treasures in heaven, where neither moth nor rust destroys, and where thieves do not break in or steal; for where your treasure is, there your heart will be also" (Matthew 6:19–21).

Earthly treasure has to be viewed as having a heavenly purpose. When our lives are transformed, we

---

7 - Ibid.

begin to view treasure as God does: as our testimony. It is a relationship with Jesus Christ. When you follow his will and "seek first the kingdom of God and his righteousness" you will then find "all these things will be added to you" (Matthew 6:33).

A Mature Look at Treasure

Usually, people's understanding of money matures as they age. Children don't know a piece of candy doesn't cost $20. Even young adults 15- or 16-years-old don't have the same view of money as when they are in their 30s or 40s. Kevin, my son mentioned earlier, is an example. He loved to work. He put the money he earned into empty tennis ball cans, one for each of three ways he used his money: spending, saving, and giving. The one for giving had 20% written on it.

Now, many kids who go to church learn to tithe; that is, to give 10 percent back to God, whether from their allowance or money earned from cutting grass or babysitting. But Kevin's giving can had *20%* on it. I asked him once how he arrived at that decision. He said, "I just want to make sure God knows how much I love him."

Now I realized that for some 20% may not be a lot. For some it may be a ton. I don't know your circumstances. But what I do know is this: that God can speak to teenage boys and get ahold of their hearts, so they want to make sure God knows how much they love him. It's about testimony. It's about what Jesus has done for us. Kevin wanted 20% on that empty can because he didn't want to have any misunderstanding about what mattered most to him. That was his way of saying, "I love God with all of my heart."

I hope Kevin's testimony encourages you to remember that Jesus is our treasure. Like Kevin, when our heart is on Jesus our treasure will follow our heart right into his kingdom.

What We can Learn from a Dollar Bill

I'd like for you to stop reading for a second and find some paper money. It might be on your person or in your home. Just take a $1 or $5 bill; it doesn't matter. But don't read any farther until you have a bill in hand. (If you can't find paper money, use a debit card, or turn on your phone's payment app.)

Now, I want you to hold that bill. I want you to look at that bill and I want you to turn it to its reverse. I want you to study it and I want you to examine it. And now I want you to think back when you made your first dollar. How old were you? Six? Eight? Eleven? Take some time if you need to.

What did you do to earn that dollar? Newspaper boy? Yard work? Weekly chores? Now let me ask you another question: what did that dollar mean to you?

We know that businesses often take their first dollar, frame it, and put it up on the wall, right? What did that dollar mean to you? How happy did it make you? I mean, wasn't it great?

I remember the first dollar I made. I had to work over two hours to do it. My grandpa paid me a penny a minute. He paid me the $1.20 in quarters and dimes. I gave 20 cents as a tithe and offering and kept the dollar. It was a test to make sure that no matter what the denominations of money were, that I would be faithful to the Lord with my giving.

I think about that dollar that I made. I don't have it anymore, of course. It's gone. It's spent. You likely don't have your first dollar either! But I want you to think about the blessing that dollar was. Wasn't it a blessing? It was an incredible blessing to have that dollar bill.

Now, fast forward to today. The bill, piece of plastic, or app you currently hold in your hand represents all the dollars that you possess. Is it more of a burden or is it still a blessing? My experience has been that, for whatever the reason might be, whether we have a lot of them or not very many, these things we hold in our hand called currency can very easily turn into a burden. They become a burden because we worry about the stock market, and we worry about investments, and we worry about debt, and we worry about college, and we worry about weddings, and we worry about house payments, and we worry about lots and lots of things.

What's interesting is that on the dollar bill we all got when we were young, we also were really given the key to what puts it in its proper place and what allows us to be able to keep this a blessing. On the back of my dollar bill it says, "In God we trust." I'm fairly certain on the back of your dollar bill it says the same thing. Proverbs 3:5, 6 says, "Trust in the Lord with all your heart. Lean not on your own understanding. In all your ways acknowledge him and he will make your path straight."

If your bills have become burdens to you, perhaps it's because you view them as treasure to be owned rather than things belonging to God that you manage. Don't let what God intended as a blessing become a burden as I've seen in so many lives throughout my years of ministry.

Now, I want you to do something very practical. Find a sticky-note or other small piece of paper. Write on it the date you are reading this. Now I want you to pray. You can use this as an example:

Lord, I'm giving to you the burden that money has caused in my life. I know that you intended to bless me. Through this season of blessing, there has also come with it a great burden for whatever the reason might be. And I release that burden to you in order that I might be able to

89

experience the fullness of your presence. I know as long as these cause a burden in my life, and my focus is on the cares of this world, I won't experience your full presence. I cast all my cares on you because you care for me. I lay this at your feet and ask that you help me leave it there until it can be a blessing again, until I can truly say, "In God I trust."

Take the time to do that. Now stick that sticky-note or paper to the bill and put it on a bookshelf or table in your room. Let it be a memorial to you. Surrender that burden to God every time you see that bill with the date on top.

Part of our Kingdom Assignment is to experience the blessing of God. If we are going to experience the presence of God and the peace of God, then there certainly needs to be a blessing from God. Be a blessing to God and others. This is how we utilize our treasure, our testimony, our talent, and our time.

The purpose of this chapter is for us to understand the place of treasure in God's kingdom. It's for us to understand the power of blessing, the fact that we are a blessing to God. If somehow we think that treasure is what's required for us to be a blessing, we miss the point of God's call upon our lives. His call upon our lives is to know him. The Kingdom Assignment is to walk with Jesus.

And what flows from there is opportunity.

A rare Ford Motor Company phone directory of employees. Henry Ford's phone number was 2, Edsel Ford's was 3.

Chapter Nine

PRINCIPLE AND PRINCIPAL

Do you remember learning about *homophones* in school? It refers to words that sound alike but have different meanings and often different spellings: *new* and *knew, no* and *know, so* and *sew,* or *to, too,* and *two*.

In this chapter I want us to look at two words that are pronounced the same but have very different meanings—especially when it comes to our priorities in life. The words are *principle* and *principal*. Among the ways the Cambridge Dictionary defines principle are *a moral rule or standard of good behavior*, and *a basic truth that explains or controls how something happens or works*. I would use *a set of values and beliefs that govern that rule, that guide, that lead my life*.

Cambridge defines principal as *an amount of money lent or borrowed*. For the contrast I'm making in this chapter, think of *a sum of money*. So, we have P-L-E and P-A-L.

What is my highest priority in life? Is it the P-L-E that expresses the set of core values that govern my life? Or does P-A-L determine the outcomes of my life, that is the money that I may or may not have? If you have somehow landed on P-A-L—whether subtly or intentionally your possessions possess you—you now have an opportunity to reset the score getting the priorities of life right.

Like the Industrialists we've returned to several times in this book, we know it's possible to allow Principle to guide your Principal. Money can be used for Kingdom purposes. The problem comes when it gets reversed, when Principal (money) takes priority over values (principle). This is what Paul addresses in 1 Timothy 6:10, "For the love of money is a root of all sorts of evil, and some by longing for it have wandered away from the faith and pierced themselves with many griefs." Keeping P-L-E before P-A-L will help you keep P-A-L in perspective no matter how much God blesses you with.

Keeping the Right Order

So how do we keep P-L-E and P-A-L in the right order? We learn from what Jesus teaches us in Matthew 6:25–34:

> Therefore I tell you, do not worry about your life, what you will eat or drink; or about your body, what you will wear. Is not life more than food, and the body more than clothes? Look at the birds of the air; they do not sow or reap or store away in barns, and yet your heavenly Father feeds them. Are you not much more valuable than they? Can any one of you by worrying add a single hour to your life? And why do you worry about clothes? See how the flowers of the field grow. They do not labor or spin. Yet I tell you that not even Solomon in all his splendor was dressed like one of these. If that is how God clothes the grass of the field, which is here today and tomorrow is thrown into the fire, will he not much more clothe you—you of little faith? So do not worry, saying, 'What shall we eat?' or 'What shall we drink?' or 'What shall we wear?' For the pagans run after all these things, and your heavenly Father knows that you need them. But seek first his kingdom and his righteousness, and all these things will be given to you as well. Therefore do not worry about tomorrow, for tomorrow will worry about itself. Each day has enough trouble of its own. (NIV)

Notice verse 33 again and ask yourself, "What are 'all these things'?" I believe it's the things that we seem to worry about, care about, and really believe that we need for life itself. You read the verses prior to it, and it'll tell you exactly to seek first the kingdom of God. We can do that on an easy day, right? But, it's harder to do on a hard day, harder to do when circumstances aren't good, harder to do when we've been dealt a blow in life. But, still Jesus says, "Seek first his kingdom and his righteousness."

That means doing what is right according to God. This isn't anything that is subjective, where my right is my right, and your right is your right. He is talking about God's righteousness. Seek first the kingdom of God and his righteousness. Then all these things will be added unto you. So let's move forward in faith, believing that God is able to take us where we are and carry us through the tomorrows of life. That's what he will do.

Living for Others

Through the power of the Spirit, we can live with an overflow so that people see the overflow and they ask about the hope that is in us. But we cannot give to others what we do not have inside of us. The former is from a reservoir of relationship; the latter is from a well gone dry called religion.

We can give to others what we have inside of our well that is a reservoir of relationship. One reason I'm so excited about this book on Transformational Living is because it's not a religion we are talking about being taught—not in any way, shape, or form. It is a relationship I am advocating. It is a relationship with Jesus Christ in which we make him premier in all that we do. And when he is, that is a fulfillment of the Kingdom Assignment.

It's also an opportunity for us to be set free to follow him where he would lead. In chapter one we talked about being ready for heaven. Then we learned it's not only about *us* being ready for heaven, but it's about helping *others* find Jesus as well. We will never help others find Jesus if we aren't willing to simply help them. Helping them opens the door to the gospel. Helping others is a way of planting seeds that can later grow and bear fruit.

I love to garden. I have one on the back of my property and look forward to working in it every year. We grow tomatoes and peppers for salsa (gotta love salsa!) and cucumbers for bread and butter pickles. We also have fruit trees: peach, cherry, apple, and pear. We love to make juice and fresh desserts, too.

God has blessed us with so many things. But here's the lesson: if you don't plant the seeds, you don't get salsa. You don't get apples. You don't get pickles. Fruit-bearing starts with seed-sowing. We can sow seed into people's lives when we help them; when we are generous in their times of need; when we pay attention to their situations and respond. Like the Samaritan man in Jesus' parable, don't cross the road to avoid the hurting like the religious leaders did. Instead, go to those in need and help.

The Role of Faith in Your Kingdom Assignment

This is true for 1st century farmers and 21st century farmers: we all plant in faith. We have to plant trusting something is happening that we can't see. We plant seeds then cover them with soil. We bury them trusting they will germinate and grow. But, we can't see it happen and we can't know for sure it's happening until that shoot comes up into the light!

That's what it's like to live by faith; it's Transformational Living. Hebrews 11 reminds us that faith is the substance of things *hoped for* and the evidence of things *not seen*. We don't see the things we're trusting God for. We don't always see what God is doing under the surface. We don't see the seeds we've planted germinating. God is doing the miraculous, but sometimes it looks to us like he isn't doing anything! That's where faith comes in. We trust God even when the seeds we've planted aren't doing anything we can see.

Hebrews 11 is often called the Great Faith Chapter or the Hall of Faith. When you read it it's easy to see why. (If you haven't read it recently, pause reading this book and reread it.) Each of the people mentioned are commended for something they did by faith. In fact, *by faith* is the phrase that introduces each new person or group of people in the chapter. Each of these things were done by faith:

- Abel offered a more acceptable sacrifice than his brother, Cain.
- Enoch was taken up to heaven without dying.
- Noah built the ark for his family, himself, and a lot of animals.
- Abraham left the land of his birth for a new homeland.
- Sarah gave birth to a child in her advanced years.
- Isaac promised blessings to his sons.
- Moses' parents hid him from Pharoah's executioners.
- Rahab hid Israel's spies.

And the list goes on. The writer says, "Time will fail" if he attempts to tell all the stories of faith that would come to his mind (v 32).

All these things done *by faith*. The New Living Translation phrases the section about Moses this way: "He kept right on going because he kept his eyes on the one who is invisible" (v 27). Doesn't that really sum up what Transformational Living is all about? Isn't keeping your eyes on the one who is invisible how you will fulfill your Kingdom Assignment?

Yes, it is.

We don't pursue our Kingdom Assignment because we already know what's going to happen. When Henry Ford first conceived of the assembly line, he didn't know how many cars would be produced. He just knew it would be more. When John Rockefeller bought his first oil well, he didn't know Standard Oil would eventually reach monopoly strength (according to the government). When J.P. Morgan invested his first dollar, he didn't know he'd one day be able to save the United States financial system.

When I started volunteering at the Oregon Youth Authority, I didn't know how many young adults would come to faith in Jesus. I didn't know how many would be baptized. I only knew God gave me a Kingdom Assignment then opened a door. I walked through it in faith. When I came to Mission Increase (the nonprofit organization that published the book you are reading), I didn't know the extent of the opportunity. I accepted it in faith. When I plant a pepper seed, I don't know how many peppers will come from the plant. That's in God's hands as he uses sun, rain, and pollinating insects. I plant in faith.

Perhaps right now you are thinking of a time in your life you needed to see him who is invisible. Maybe it's a decision you need to make right now. May I remind you what is at stake? People are lost and need the Lord.

Lord, please help us! Please help us to always remember that our message is one of great, great hope and one that every person on earth needs to hear. Help us to accept our Kingdom Assignments so you can use us to plant seeds all over the world that will grow and bear Kingdom fruit.

Faith Is the Key

In the Revelation given to the Apostle John, Jesus says to the church of Philadelphia, "I know your works. Behold, I have set before you an open door, which no one is able to shut. I know that you have but little power, and yet you have kept my word and have not denied my name" (3:8).

Maybe sometimes you feel like you have little power. You aren't as influential as you'd like to be and maybe the promotions at work have come slower than you wish. Jesus says the most important thing is to keep his word and not deny his name. If you do that, he will honor you.

As a practical reminder, I want to invite you to do this: the next time you are near a hardware store or a big-box store with a key-making center, stop and buy a blank key. Put it on your key ring as a matter of faith. As you continue through *Transformational Living: Discover Your Kingdom Assignment* and beyond, there will be an open door that God's going to place you in front of. When you see that open door, you may think, "I've never seen that door? What's on the other side?"

That's when this key reminds you to walk in faith. The Holy Spirit will cut all the grooves that need to be made. When that door is open, the Holy Spirit is leading you all the way. You don't go ahead of the Holy Spirit; the Holy Spirit goes ahead of you.

So let his key be a key of faith! Remember the dollar bill from the last chapter? It tells you the burden is gone and the blessing has come. Now the key encourages us to go through the door that God has opened.

We say, "Yes. Here I am. Send me."

Still standing today on 57th and 7th Avenue in New York City is Carnegie Hall paid for by Andrew Carnegie. It opened on May 5, 1891.

CONCLUSION

It is my prayer that this book has been as much a blessing to you in reading it as it was to me in researching and writing it. In all the times I've taught this material in live settings, it never fails to bless me. Knowing that God provides himself as the basis for living transformed lives is amazing. Getting to participate with his kingdom's work is outstanding.

What a great God we serve!

As we conclude this study, I want to address the two groups of people reading. Many of you already know Jesus; you have already entered the kingdom of God through faith in the Son of God, Jesus Christ. Praise God! Others of you are still seeking or thinking or praying that God will help you somehow. I want to talk to the second group first.

There's a passage of scripture in John's gospel that records some of the words Jesus spoke during his suffering. Jesus is on the cross. Jesus is about to complete the work that his Father had given him. John writes,

Jesus, knowing that all things had already been accomplished, to fulfill the Scripture, said, 'I am thirsty.' A jar full of sour wine was standing there; so they put a sponge full of the sour wine upon a branch of hyssop and brought it up to His mouth. Therefore when Jesus had received the sour wine, He said, 'It is finished!' And He bowed His head and gave up His spirit. (John 19:28–30)

Jesus was actually preparing the people of the world—you, me, all generations—for the greatest reset in human history. Jesus was preparing himself and all who would follow him for heaven. Transformational Living begins with salvation; it begins with redemption. So let me ask you this question, do you have a personal relationship with Jesus? If, as you were reading this book, you wondered whether you would have a Kingdom Assignment, I can tell you it follows trusting Jesus, coming into a relationship with him.

The Bible teaches that we are born not as children of God, but as ones separated from him. If you remember from chapter one, we talked about several scriptures that deal with salvation.

- Everyone is born as a sinner (Romans 3:23).
- The wages of sin is death, but God offers eternal life in Jesus (Romans 6:23).
- Jesus is knocking on your heart's door seeking to enter and fellowship with you (Revelation 3:20).
- For everyone who does receive Jesus, who believe on his name, are made children of God (John 1:12).
- Because God loves the world, he gave his only son, Jesus Christ, to save everyone who believes (John 3:16).

If you do not know Jesus as your personal savior, stop reading at this point. Pray. Tell God you are sorry for your sins and that you "repent," that is, you're turning away from your sinful life and turning to Jesus. In faith, ask God to forgive you, save you, and make you his child. Now, thank him for the new life he has given you!

I rejoice with you that you are now a child of God through Jesus!

What's Next?

For those of you who just accepted Jesus and to those of you who were already saved, you are prime candidates to move into Transformational Living. Why wouldn't you want to discover your Kingdom Assignment so you can make a great difference in this life and the life to come?

In the Old Testament book of Joshua 24:15 we read, "Choose this day whom you will serve." Note the urgency, the immediacy. Choose "this day." There is a clear sense that this is something that shouldn't be put off, that shouldn't be delayed. You need to take care of this as soon as possible. Finding your Kingdom Assignment is not a matter of national security; no, it's more important than that. It's a matter of eternal consequence.

To help you, I recorded nine teaching sessions that match the chapters in this book. Mission Increase has developed a workbook that includes everything you need to get the most out of this study. It's designed to use with the videos for the greatest impact.

Although you can do the study by yourself with a study partner or mentor, I recommend doing it as a group. The feedback, encouragement, and combined learning can't be beat! Mission Increase even created a leader guide to help facilitate the discussion.

There are two components to the workbook designed to specifically help you find your Kingdom Assignment. First is the "Kingdom Business Plan, then the guide 30-Days Toward Your Kingdom Assignment." These are to be used together, working back and forth as you seek God's will for your Kingdom Assignment. For thirty days you'll be in God's word, then praying, thinking about your head, hands, and heart, as you journal what God is doing in your life.

Of course, it's possible to do this study alone, but I don't recommend that. Other believers can help you along this journey—and you can help them. That's why I think a group study holds the most value. But if there aren't enough people at your church going through *Transformational Living: Discover Your Kingdom Assignment Workbook*, then find a trusted mentor to work through it together. Either way, don't let this book be the end of your journey. Make it the beginning.

A word to those of you who are married: The process of completing your Kingdom Assignment begins at home. It begins with your family. You and your spouse need to agree on both of your Kingdom Assignments. Then, you need to bring your family along, especially if you have younger children who will be affected by God's call on your life.

If I Could Do It Again

What you have read and are getting ready to study is something I wish had been available to me as a younger Christian. It would have helped me greatly. In fact, this has come about through a lifetime of saying to myself, "If I could do this all over again, how could I make a difference in the Kingdom?" One of the ways God has called me to make a difference is helping people discover their Kingdom Assignment and complete that assignment within the framework of a transformed life. Then what's most important to Jesus is most important to us, so that his will is done on earth as it is in heaven.

As you come to the close of this book, I want to pray for you.

Father, we want to serve you and have an opportunity to follow in the footsteps of Jesus. We want to impact your kingdom for your glory. We want to help people know Jesus. Help each person reading to experience transformed living. Help them to find and complete their Kingdom Assignment. And help them yield their time, talent, treasure, and influence for your kingdom. Please Holy Spirit lead each of us in the way you would have us go until your kingdom comes in its fullness. Amen.

To Learn More

Transformational Living: Discover Your Kingdom Assignment is also available for individual and group study with Randy Butler's online video instruction and Workbook/Leader's Guide bundles. Both the Workbook and Leader's Guide include 9-weeks of study notes, a template to develop your Kingdom Business Plan, a self-guided devotional entitled "30-Days Toward Your Kingdom Assignment", biographical sketches of the five industrialists, and a full bibliography of over 100 books. Visit MissionIncrease.org for more information or to order *Transformational Living* bundles for your church or group.

To schedule Randy for a weekend of teaching *Transformational Living* live at your church, or for your leadership team retreat, or business leaders' group, visit missionincrease.org/transformational-living or scan the QR code below.

SCAN ME

Spiritual Biographical Sketches of Vanderbilt, Rockefeller, Carnegie, Morgan, and Ford

I was at home minding my own business one evening in 2012, when Joanie, my wife, exclaimed, "Randy, you need to come in here and see this."

I responded something like, "I'm busy and don't have time."

She replied with even greater urgency, "You really need to come in here and see this. It's what you've been talking about recently."

I broke away from what I was doing, walked to the other room, sat down and within minutes I was mesmerized. My heart began to swell up with something that seemed almost like a revival in my soul. I took notes, realizing God was moving in my life in a profound way, taking me on a journey has led me to you today. This book is one of many stops as I live life with the industrialists the History Channel called, The Men Who Built America.

Since that first viewing of the series, I was compelled to study, research, and learn all I could about these five men: Cornelius Vanderbilt, John D. Rockefeller, Andrew Carnegie, John Pierpont (J.P.) Morgan, and Henry Ford.

The book excerpts that follow show evidence of the influence of Christianity on these five men. You will discover the profound impact their pastors and their churches had on them. Vanderbilt was converted to Christ later in life and afterwards was moved to purchase a building for his church.

Though most of these pastors' names are lost to history, their influence on each of their respective industrialist member was immense.

- Charles Deems was pastor and personal advisor to Cornelius Vanderbilt
- Fred Gates was pastor and personal advisor to John D. Rockefeller
- Henry Sloan Coffin was Andrew Carnegie's pastor
- William S. Rainsford was J.P. Morgan's pastor
- Samuel Marquis as pastor and personal advisor to Henry Ford (and an employee)

In addition to pastors, the following women played significant roles in their homes and marriages, while influencing the spirituality and generosity of their husbands.

- Frank Howard (Vanderbilt's second wife)
- Laura "Cettie" Spelman (Rockefeller's wife)
- Louise Whitfield (Carnegie's wife)
- Francis Louise Tracy (Morgan's second wife)
- Clara Bryant (Ford's wife)

I've chosen to present the following excerpts by book rather than by theme, sequential order, or perceived importance. The reader is invited to look at the evidence in its total sum and discover the impact God had on these industrialists' lives. The Bible and their faith in God helped to shape their business and philanthropy philosophies, their economic theologies, and their decision-making processes.

As mentioned earlier, I developed *Transformational Living: Discover Your Kingdom Assignment* over a decade of study partially based on the lives of these industrialists. Finding gold nuggets does not come easily, but after these years of mining their lives, I'm happy to share what I've unearthed with you.

I've been a licensed minister since 1980, pastored several churches, and have done many memorial services and celebrations of life. Never have I heard negative remarks shared about the life of the person being memorialized. Yet, for these five—Vanderbilt, Rockefeller, Carnegie, Morgan, and Ford—much criticism was leveled at them when they were alive and in some cases, even sharper criticism after their death. I am aware of how these five men have been painted throughout history. It is my privilege to share their faith in God. Are they perfect? No! They are human beings who were ordained by God to change the world, and in so doing, they accumulated vast sums of money, much of which was deployed into the Kingdom during their lifetime and beyond.

Imagine for a moment that you have just entered a memorial service in a local church. You received a bulletin, signed the guest book, and have taken a seat in the sanctuary. The service is about to begin. You are sitting in a church built with supplies that came via railroads, thanks to Vanderbilt. Your gas- or diesel-powered car is fueled, compliments of Rockefeller. You may have safely driven over a steel bridge on the way to the church, courtesy of Carnegie. The reader had the financial means to attend, partially thanks to Morgan. Finally, you drove your car to the memorial service, in part, thanks to Ford.

Our lives have already intersected with these five great industrialists. On the following pages, explore the influence Christianity had on them. So, as the late radio host Paul Harvey used to say, "And now, the rest of the story…"

Cornelius "Commodore" Vanderbilt (1794-1877)
Commodore Vanderbilt: An Epic of American Achievement
by Arthur D. Howden Smith

She never got him to church, but she did succeed in introducing a clergyman as a regular visitor to the household and ultimately made this person, Rev. Charles F. Deems, his intimate advisor. Her greatest achievement, probably, was in persuading him to reverse his dictum against charity. Dr. Deems is usually credited with inducing him to make this departure from his lifelong rule, but Mrs. Frank must have been the silent mainspring of the kindly conspiracy. Surely, Corneel would never have given $50,000 to buy the Church of the Strangers for Deems without suggestions having been made in the home circle. And while it is true that Deems brought him in touch with Southern clergymen who were agitating the educational needs of their war-torn region, his wife's descriptions of the South's sufferings were certainly a factor in carrying him to the point of giving $1,000,000 to found and endow Vanderbilt University. However, you regard it, Mrs. Frank was a force to be reckoned with. If she lacked the shrewd and pungent personality of Phoebe Hand and the self-effacing devotion of Sophia, she nursed and tended a crotchety, fierce, old man, who was dreaded in his periodic rages by all who must approach him, and gentled him into paths of humility he had never trod before. She deserves her place in the small gallery of women who molded his character. (p. 304-305)

Memorial tablet erected to the late Commodore Vanderbilt in the Church the Strangers, New York City…Erected to the Glory of God and in memory of Cornelius Vanderbilt by the Church of the Strangers… He was worthy for he hath built us a synagogue. (p. 309)

Thinking on the subject, and with his young wife and Dr. Deems ready to spur his inward scrutiny, he became mildly religious. He didn't go to church, as did eighty percent of Americans in that churchgoing era, but he liked to hear and participate in religious discussion at home. (p. 318)

Of books he knew nothing at all, except for the dog-eared copy of Pilgrim's Progress which his wife had given him. (p. 319)

Religion, as his wife and Dr. Deems taught it, had weaned him finally from spiritualism. (p. 328)

He was glad to have lived in such interesting times. He noticed, in the excitement of the holidays, that the Shadow seemed to have lifted slightly, and for a day or so he felt lighthearted; but then he realized his foolishness, and chuckled, in his quiet, grim way, to himself. Joke was on him, b' God. Hold on, he might cuss. Jesus was his friend,

Deems said. Frank believed it, too. Call on Jesus, they said. (p. 329)

On January 3, he was so well that he sat up, and talked to his callers, but after he returned to bed that night, he felt strange. Frank came hastily, Billy and the gals and their husbands. Linsley was there, and three or four more doctors. Deems entered towards morning, quiet-footed, deferential. The clergyman talked to Mrs. Crawford, Frank's mother (Frank was the wife of Vanderbilt) standing by the bed foot, and Corneel beckoned to them weakly. "Sing," he whispered, "hymn." Mrs. Crawford raised her voice, and one by one the rest joined in, "Come ye sinners, poor and needy," they sang and when he signed for more, "Nearer My God to Thee" and "Show Pity, Lord." He asked for Dr. Deems to pray, listening avidly as the words fell from the clergyman's lips. "That's a good prayer," he murmured. His fingers groped out, and fastened upon Deems's hand. "I'll never give up trust in Jesus," he quavered. "How could I let that go?" The Shadow settled over him like a blanket, cool, soothing, pleasantly restful. Rest, that was what he needed. (p. 330-331)

John D. Rockefeller (1839-1937)
Toward the Well-Being of Mankind
by Robert Shaplen

Gates, a fervid evangelist, who, as Fosdick adds, "could never be anything but candid and forthright" is reported to have thundered at the elder Rockefeller, "your fortune is rolling up, rolling up like an avalanche. You must keep up with it! You must distribute it faster than it grows! If you do not, it will crush you and your children and your children's children!" (p. 5)

Random Reminiscences of Men and Events
by John D. Rockefeller

The education of children in my early days may have been straightlaced, yet I have always been thankful that the custom was quite general to teach young people to give systematically of money that they themselves have earned. (p. 146)

Up to the present time no scheme has yet presented itself which seems to afford a better method of handling capital than that of individual ownership. We might put our money into the Treasury of the Nation and of the various states, but we do not find any promise in the National or state legislatures, viewed from the experiences of the past, that the funds would be expended for the general weal more effectively than under the present methods, nor do we find any of the schemes of socialism a promise that wealth would be more wisely administered for the general good. (p.159-160)

If a combination to do business is effective in saving waste and in getting better results, why is not combination far more important in philanthropic work? The general idea of a cooperation in giving for education, I have felt, scored a real step in advance when Mr. Andrew Carnegie consented to become a member of the General Education Board. For in accepting a position in this directorate he has, it seems to me, stamped with his approval this vital principle of cooperation in aiding the education institutions of our country. (p. 165)

Doctors, clergymen, lawyers, as well as many high-grade men of affairs, are devoting their best and most unselfish efforts to some of the plans we are all trying to work out. (p. 167)

Dear Father/Dear Son
by Joseph W. Ernst

Sept 24, 1893
Dear Father,
Our class is the largest which had ever entered college, and numbers about 175. Grandmother will be interested to know that there are three colored men in the class. We had a class prayer meeting the other afternoon, and you would have been much pleased with the spirit exhibited. Before the meeting was over, all the men from the three other class prayer meetings came in a single file singing "Blessed be the tie that binds," and while they sang they walked through one line of seats and then another, and every one of them shook hands with every man in our class. Then they all stood around, and one of them prayed, and then said a few words about the responsibility resting on each one of us, and the amount of good that a band of fellows could do if they would stand together. (p. 11)

January 18, 1909
Dear Son,
I thank you a thousand times for the fur coat and cap and mittens. I did not feel that I could afford such luxuries and am grateful for a son who is able to buy them for me. Be assured they are much appreciated. (p. 30)

March 17, 1909
Dear Father,
The monetary value of these gifts is of course tremendous, running into a number of millions of dollars and I do not for a moment underestimate its proportions. But to me their greatest worth lies in the fact that they give evidence of your deep confidence in me and in my earnest purpose under God to use my life and my opportunities and my possessions as my Heavenly Father may direct and my earthly parents would approve. This confidence I prize above all else, and to merit such approval do I daily strive. (p. 35)

February 11, 1919
Dear Father,
May the God who has led you so wonderfully during all of these years of your life, whom you have served so faithfully and untiringly, lead me in the same path of duty and of service and help me to carry on worthily the works for mankind which with marvelous provision you have so solidly and wisely established. (p. 90)

By 1922 Senior had given Junior over $465 million. The large gifts were made between 1916 and 1922… (p. 225)

John D. Rockefeller and his son John D. Rockefeller Jr., shared in the adventure once described by Senior as an effort toward making a better world. This is the legacy of their understanding of their stewardship. (p. 229)

John D. Rockefeller: The Cleveland Years
by Grace Goulder

Remembering His Bible's warnings about pride and its dangers, he declared he seldom put his head "upon the pillow at night without speaking a few words to myself." What he termed, "these intimate conversations with myself" came to be more or less habitual throughout his life. He was thus enabled "to stand prosperity" and was saved from getting "puffed up" as he put it. His religion was a practical religion as befitted to a practical man.

He used his Bible freely like a tool. (p. 45)

Perhaps it was at anti-slavery meetings that Rockefeller renewed his acquaintance with Laura Celestia Spelman- "Cettie" to her classmates, and "Cettie" to John. The Spelmans were ardent abolitionists. Rockefeller, too, it would seem was driven early into the crusade judging from his gifts to negro causes. (p. 62)

Later as Mrs. John D. Rockefeller, she took no part in her husband's business affairs. As appeals for help mounted, Rockefeller's giving reflected his wife's point of view as much as his own. (p. 66)

Always committed to go to Sunday morning and evening Church. (p. 71)

From his marriage on, John D. made his wife a partner in his giving. (p. 104)

He was no novice in the role of chairman, for he had learned the art as a teen-ager when appointed head of the Erie Street Church's board of trustees, all older than he. Except for Colonel Payne, the Standard's new directors were also his seniors. (p. 115)

With these events swirling about him, his church was never neglected. He took his place as a superintendent of the Sunday School at the Euclid Avenue Baptist Church and made notes about the sermon for Laura if she was unable to attend. (p. 120)

John and Laura Rockefeller seemed more concerned with their children's spiritual than with their physical wellbeing. (p. 123)

The Rockefellers' purpose this time was to see their daughter, Mrs. Charles Strong (Bessie) who was ill, suffering from a nervous malady in which she was obsessed with the fear of dying in poverty. (p. 201)

Memoirs
by David Rockefeller

"...to promote the wellbeing of mankind throughout the world." (p. 210)

Standard Oil made Grandfather rich, possibly "the richest man in America." He was also, for much of his life, one of the most hated. The tabloid press attacked Standard's business practices and accused it of crimes-including murder...

Grandfather was the target of Progressives, Populists, Socialists, and other discontented with the new American capitalist order...

Robert La Follette, the powerful governor of Wisconsin, called him the "greatest criminal of his age..."

Ida Tarbell, who through her writings probably did more than anyone to establish the image of Grandfather as greedy and rapacious "robber baron," wrote, "There is little doubt that Mr. Rockefeller's chief reason for playing golf is that he may live longer to make more money." (p. 5)

In my view it was my Grandfather's deep religious faith that gave him his placid self-assurance in the face of personal attacks, and supreme confidence that enabled him to consolidate the American oil industry. He was a devout Christian who lived by the strict tenets of his Baptist faith. His faith "explained" the world around him on his way through it and provided him with a liberating structure. The most important of these principles was that faith without good works was meaningless. That central belief led Grandfather to first accept the "doctrine of stewardship" for his great fortune and then to broaden it by creating the great philanthropies later in life. (p. 7)

Beyond Charity: A Century of Philanthropic Innovation
by Eric John Abrahamson, Ph.D.

Rockefeller's interest in the welfare of African Americans at an early stage in his philanthropy was no doubt strengthened by his marriage to Laura Celestia Spelman in 1864. "Cettie," as her friends called her, had grown up in a deeply religious Congregationalist household in Cleveland, where her parents were active abolitionists and supporters of the Underground Railroad. She was an early supporter of the temperance movement as well. (p. 41)

Junior, born on January 29, 1874, shared many of his father's traits but also was profoundly influenced by his mother's homeschooling. As the only son among four children who survived infancy, Junior learned from his mother the spirit and precepts of the New Testament. The family prayed, read the Bible, and recited verses on a daily basis. Every Friday night they attended prayer meeting. They respected Sunday as a day of rest and devotion. (p. 45)

Senior and Junior were both moved to philanthropy by religious views derived from the Puritan traditions of New England. In the Puritan view the faithful were bound to one another by God's love. Charity was a manifestation of that love. (p. 47)

High status or wealth, however, did not accrue to the individual, but to "the glory of his Creator and the common good of the creature, man." Thus the wealth and powerful were seen by the community and should be seen by themselves as God's stewards. (p. 47)

Junior was profoundly influenced by his parents' faith as well as the crisis of Protestantism in the late nineteenth century that was prompted by the second scientific and industrial revolution. In the context of the challenge raised by Darwin and others, believers sought to reconcile the Bible with the understandings of science. (p. 48)

Like their Puritan forefathers, Senior and Junior worked assiduously to turn their high ideals into ordinary realities. Both men subscribed to the Puritan notion of two callings: one to a godly life and the other to a specific vocation. For Junior, especially, that vocation was philanthropy. (p. 48)

Born in 1853, Gates was the son of a New York Baptist preacher. At age fifteen, he had become a schoolteacher to help his family pay its bills. Gates confessed to being repulsed by the repressive Puritan faith of his parents when he was a boy. Yet, for Gates, like Rockefeller, this Puritan heritage would have a profound influence on his view of the world. Graduating from the Rochester Theological Seminary, a Baptist institution, Gates moved to Minneapolis to become a pastor at the Fifth Avenue Baptist Church. (p. 56–57)

Gates met George Pillsbury, the flour magnate, and got his first taste of advising the wealthy on their philanthropy when Pillsbury came to him regarding a bequest he intended to make to support a Baptist academy in Minnesota. In 1888, Gates was picked to lead the American Baptist Education Society, with a primary goal of developing a great university in Chicago. (p. 57)

Andrew Carnegie (1835-1919)
My Own Story
by Andrew Carnegie

My power to memorize must have been greatly strengthened by the mode of teaching adopted by my uncle. I cannot name a more important means of benefiting young people than encouraging them to commit favorite pieces to memory and recite them often.

One of the trials of my boy's life at school in Dunfermline was committing to memory two double verses of the Psalms which I had to recite daily. My plan was not to look at the Psalm until I had started for school. It was not more than five or six minutes' slow walk, but I could readily master the task in that time, and, as the Psalm was the first lesson, I was prepared and passed through the ordeal successfully. (p. 9)

Triumphant Democracy
by Andrew Carnegie

At the time of the Revolution (1776) there were one thousand four-hundred and sixty-one ministers and one thousand nine-hundred and fifty-one churches, which gave one minister for every two thousand and fifty three souls and a church for every one thousand five hundred and thirty-eight. In 1880 there was a minister for every six-hundred and sixty and a church for every five hundred and fifty-three. Wherever the American settles he begins at once the erection of his schoolhouse and his church. (p. 157–158)

The evils of the State Church flow from its parent, the Monarchy, of which it is the legitimate offspring. Its archbishops and bishops residing in palaces and rolling in wealth are the religious aristocracy; the thousands of poor curates who drag out existence upon pittances represent the masses. The revenues of the State Church exceed five million pounds sterling. The Church owns all kinds of property and is squeamish about none. (p. 161)

Without Church-rate or tithe, without State endowment or state supervision, religion in America has spontaneously acquired a strength which no political support could have given it. It is a living force entering into the lives of the people and drawing them closer together in unity of feeling, and working silently and without sign of the friction which in the mother country results from a union with the State, which, as we have seen, tends strongly to keep the people divided one from another. The power of the church in America must not be sought as, Burke said of an ideal aristocracy, "in rotten parchments, under dripping and perishing walls, but in full vigor, and acting with vital energy and power, in the character of the leading men and natural interests of the country." Even if judged by the church accommodation provided and the sums spent upon church organizations, Democracy can safely claim that of all the divisions of the English-speaking people, it has produced the most religious community yet known. (p. 164)

Andrew Carnegie: The Man and His Work
by Barnard Alderson

He [Carnegie] describes the parson to suit him to be one who says little and does much. He has, however, very great faith in the refining and elevating influence of music, which he speaks of as heaven's chief medium. (p. 104)

Rich men, he says, have cause to be thankful for one inestimable boon- "they have in their power, during their lives, to busy themselves in organizing benefactions from which the masses of their fellows will derive lasting benefit, and thus they will dignify their own lives." (p. 139)

Mr. Carnegie thinks this new era in the world's history has already dawned; and as the light becomes more distinct he prophecies that the voice of the people will strongly condemn the man who hoards wealth instead of wisely allotting it to better his fellow man. Making handsome bequests before the last hour will not earn the full reward. Giving during his life, in his opinion, the only just and proper course. (p. 142)

Mr. Carnegie has given his gospel the best possible christening, and there are significant signs that he is likely to have many worthy followers. While millions are a burden to some men, and crush both soul and energy, he finds in them no source of anxiety. They are his, and yet they are not. Their disbursement will give him the greatest happiness and abolish all thoughts of anxiety from his mind. (p. 141)

In the course of the article Mr. Carnegie dealt with the seven objects which, in his opinion, were worthy of the attention of those possessed of wealth.

1. To found or enlarge a university.
2. The erection of free libraries.
3. Establishment of hospitals or laboratories.
4. To present public parks.
5. To open public halls with organs.
6. To start swimming baths.
7. To build churches. (p. 145)

Churches as fields for surplus wealth have purposely been reserved until the last, because these being sectarian, every man will be governed by his own attachments; therefore it may be said gifts to churches are not in one sense gifts to the community at large, but to special classes. The millionaire should not figure how cheaply this structure can be built, but how perfect it can be made. But, having given the building, the donor should stop there; the support of the church should be upon its own people. There is not much genuine religion in the congregation or much good to flow from the church which is not supported at home. (p. 147)

Mr. Carnegie concluded his article on "The Best Fields of Philanthropy" with the following impressive declaration: "The Gospel of Wealth but echoes Christ's words; it calls upon the millionaire to sell all he hath and give the highest and the best to the poor, by administering his estate for his fellow men before he is called to lie down and rest upon the bosom of mother earth. So doing he will approach his end no longer the ignoble hoarder of useless millions; poor, very poor indeed in money, but rich, very rich in the affection, gratitude and admiration of his fellow men, and sweeter far, soothed and sustained by the still sweet voice within, which whispering tells him that because he has lived perhaps one small portion of the great world has bettered just a little. This much is sure, against such riches as these no bar will be found at the gates of Paradise." (p. 149)

Specialization began the root of individualism. Then came exchange of products, but after a time barter ceased, and certain articles—wampum, beads, skins, shells—became "money," in which were invested the savings of men. Then was slowly developed, in due progress of time, that beneficiate gospel, "as a man soweth, so shall he reap" (Galatians 6:7)—reward according to service. Many things hitherto held in common became private property. And at last, out of the savings of men (capital), durable things were built, and civilization dawned. Even in our own time not a ton nor a yard of anything can be produced, not a ship nor railroad, not a house, school, university, nor a church built without drawing upon stored-up capital, which is wealth. (p. 13)

The writer lived his early years among workmen and his later years as an employer of labor, and it is incomprehensible to him how any informed man, having at heart the elevation of manual laboring men, could fail to place upon the habit of thrift the highest value, second only to that of temperance, without which no honorable career is possible, for against intemperance no combination of good qualities can prevail. Temperance and thrift are virtues which act and react upon each other, strengthening both, and are seldom found apart. (p. 99)

This is our God-like mission, that every individual in his day and generation push on this march upward, so that each succeeding generation may be better than the preceding. Not one of us can feel his duty done, unless he can say as he approaches his end, that, because he has lived some fellow creature, or some little spot on earth or something upon it, has been made just a little better. (p. 154)

A Carnegie Anthology
by Margaret B. Wilson

When my country calls for assistance of any kind, I consider it my glorious duty to answer that call. And if the present President should command me to do anything for my country, I should regard it the same as I would the voice of God. (p. 2)

The writer, when traveling round the world, saw nothing that saddened him more than the rival sects of Christians, engaged in proclaiming their respective differences, trying to convert the heathen to a revelation about which they could not agree themselves even so far as to unite in worshipping the same God in the same temple, each sect building its own. (p. 5)

Religion is the highest expression of which a people is capable. There is no reason why we should not try to prepare a people for a better one, but note this, they must be prepared. To force new religions upon anyone is a sad mistake. (p. 9)

In the happiest and holiest homes of today, it is not the man who leads the wife upward, but the infinitely purer and more angelic wife whom the husband reverently follows upon the heavenly path as the highest embodiment of all virtues that have been revealed to him: he for God in her. Throughout the English-speaking race as a rule today, it is the wife and mother who sanctifies the home. (p. 27)

The greatest force is no longer that of brutal war which sows the seeds of future wars, but the supreme force of gentleness and generosity—the golden rule. (p. 70)

What the cross is to the Christian the idol is to the other, and it is nothing more. The worship of both is the Unknown beyond. (p. 76)

Still there is a wide providence for faith. If it does not exactly remove mountains nowadays, it at least enables us to tunnel them, which is much the same thing as far as practical results are concerned. (p. 78)

Two women, my mother and my wife, have made me all that I am. (p. 78)

Theological minds may see in the music suggested an unworthy intruder in domains sacred to dogma; but they should remember that the Bible tells us that in heaven music is the principal source of happiness—the sermon seems nowhere—and it may go hard with such as fail to give it the first place on earth. (p. 136)

The reverend gentleman said that in an ideal Christian community a millionaire would be an impossibility, to which I took the liberty of saying in reply that it was a far guess ahead just what would exist in an ideal community; but one thing was certain, that at least no preacher would be required. (p. 157)

The aspiration of a people for the God-given right to govern themselves is rarely quenched. (p. 170)

Miscellaneous Writings of Andrew Carnegie
by Burton J. Hendrick

The millionaire as such has, then, a right to his place in the world, and has no occasion to be ashamed: thus far he serves God in his time and place. (p. 134–135)

It is a growing belief with me that in the not distant future increasing importance will be attached to one truth until it overshadows all others and proves the center around which the religious sentiments will finally gather—the declaration of Christ, "The Kingdom of Heaven is within you." This was the first of several truths inscribed upon the frieze of my library in New York many years ago; there they remain and on the library frieze at Skibo there they shall be inscribed. (p. 316)

Perhaps you will see and suggest that the best test of fitness for a heavenly life hereafter and the strongest assurance of one, is that they have developed the elements of such a life here upon earth, and that unless in some degree the Kingdom of Heaven is within him here, man hopes in vain for heaven beyond. (p. 316–317) So believing, he stands awe-stricken in the holy presence of the Eternal which makes for righteousness, fearing nothing, asking nothing and, grateful for the manifold blessings already received, he reverently bows his head and murmurs his only prayer, one of self-effacement and resignation "Thy will be done." (p. 319)

John Pierpont Morgan (1837-1913)
J. Pierpont Morgan
by Herbert L. Satterlee

1883

Although he was so busy during this year, he had joined the New York Yacht Club and began to take an active interest in its affairs.

He also became a member of a committee to establish libraries and reading rooms for the use of workingmen in various parts of the city. He was unremitting in his attention to the affairs of St. George's Church and was still on the lookout for a new rector. Finally, he met William S. Rainsford, a young clergyman who had made a pronounced success in Toronto as a revivalist. Rainsford was forceful and fearless, with a most attractive personality, and had become very popular as a preacher. This first meeting, late in the autumn of 1882, resulted in Pierpont's asking Mr. Rainsford to consider coming to St. George's Church and he outlined his program for organizing the affairs of the church. He also told Mr.

Rainsford that as rector he would have a free hand in running the church, and that he, Pierpont, would find the money to carry out the plans to which they had agreed. (p. 210)

1883
It was with great satisfaction that he had Mr. Johnson install a complete electric light equipment in the rectory of St. George's Church for his friend Dr. Rainsford, and also in the church gymnasium which was much used by the young men and boys of the congregation. (p. 215)

1886
On April 3, he was elected a member of the Board of Trustees of the Cathedral of St. John the Divine, and at once took an active part in raising money for the Building Fund. However, he continued to give a great deal of time to the affairs of St. George's Church, and enthusiastically backed up Dr. Rainsford in his many enterprises to help the people of the East Side in their daily lives. (p. 236)

1889
In October, Pierpont sat as a delegate in the Triennial Convention of the Episcopal Church, which was held that year in St. George's on Stuyvesant Square. He had given a great deal of time to the preparation for this gathering, making arrangements for the seating of the delegates

in the church, giving them daily lunch during the three weeks' session and lodging and entertaining them. Moreover, his committee on the revision of the Prayer Book made its report. (p. 251)

1890

During the preceding winter Mr. Morgan had become interested in Dr. Rainsford's idea of providing a place out of town where women and children could go for relief from the city's heat during the summer months. This spring he bought and presented to the church a plot in Rockaway Park Long Island; and on this St. George's "Cottage-by the-Sea" was built. It was designed so that about fifty mothers and babies could spend a week or two there, with ample dressing rooms for bathers who came down for the day. John Reichert and his wife were put in charge, and it has been a godsend to many a poor woman who otherwise could not have got out of the city with her children in the hot season. (p. 255)

1901

On Christmas morning he and all his family were at St. George's Church as usual. There was a great crowd, as the Christmas Carols were sung and Dr. Rainsford was at the height of his popularity as a preacher. After the service Mr. Morgan called on intimate friends to wish them a Merry Christmas and, of course, went in for a few minutes to see the presents at the Hamiltons' and the Satterlees'. (p. 367-368)

1902
The house included not only living quarters for the deaconesses and the consultation and conference rooms, but rooms where women and girls who were tired could find rest and refreshment and other rooms where convalescents who had been discharged from a hospital could get back their strength before returning to work. It goes without saying that the house was of great usefulness in the parish. The building cost Mr. Morgan about $100,000. No one remembers how much he paid for the two lots. (p. 375)

1905
In September Mr. Morgan completed plans for establishing the trade-school of St. George's Church in permanent quarters. Dr. Rainsford had long felt that the best way to keep boys off the street and out of mischief was to keep them busy and years before he had started a trade-school in temporary quarters...

For years the school was operated with great success. (p. 426)

The Great Pierpont Morgan
by Frederick Lewis Allen

Along with thrift went godliness: church attendance twice on Sundays, family hymn-singing Sunday evenings, and the building of a robust religious faith, which was destined to stand almost unmodified throughout his life.

Long afterward Morgan's friend, Dr. William S. Rainsford, the rector of St. George's Church in New York, wrote that Morgan's faith was like a "precious heirloom"- "talent to be wrapped in its own napkin and venerated in the secret place of his soul...in safe disuse." (p. 12)

The first thing Morgan ever collected in his youth, aside from stamps, was the autographs of the Episcopal Bishops. He went on to become not only a formidably successful banker, but a tireless vestryman and church warden, a giver of parish houses and cathedral chapels, an energetic attender of triennial Episcopal Conventions. (p. 13)

The nature and manner of his giving followed a highly personal pattern. In the first place, many of his gifts went quite unpublicized. (You may recall his setting up a trust fund for Dr. Rainsford and telling him to mention it only to Mrs. Rainsford.) None of them involved naming a building for him. Morgan felt that a gentleman should not advertise his benefactions. The chief reason why it is so difficult for a biographer to estimate whether the total of Morgan's gifts was near five million or ten million was that so many of them were made so quietly. (p. 149)

When in the skeptical year 1913 he died, and his will was made public, those who had known him only by reputation gasped at the way in which the document began; how on earth could this monarch of Wall Street, this worldly yachtsman, this lordly spender of millions, have written those tremendous introductory words?—"I commit my soul into the hands of my Savior, in full confidence that having redeemed it and washed it in his most precious blood He will present it faultless before my Heavenly Father; and I entreat my children to maintain and defend, at all hazard and at any cost of personal sacrifice, the blessed doctrine of the complete atonement for sin through the blood of Jesus Christ, once offered, and through that alone. (p. 13)

Henry Ford (1863-1947)
My Philosophy of Industry
by Henry Ford

We should never be fearful of the cost of the right thing. (p. 29)

There was a word once spoken which throws light on this: "Seek ye first the kingdom of God and His righteousness and all these things shall be added unto you." This is from the Sermon on the Mount. It sounds religious but it is just a plain statement of facts. It means just what it says—the reign, the rule, the law of the highest relations. Get that right way, work by that, and you have the world—a world without poverty, without injustice, without need. (p. 38)

The two great hindrances to success are fear and pride. (p. 81)

People who can see the signs of the times begin their own reformation. Charity is no substitute for reform. Poverty is not cured by charity; it is only relieved. Nothing does more to abolish poverty than work. It is not the men who are doing the talking who are solving our problems, but the men who are at work. Idleness warps the mind. (p. 104-105)

Henry Ford: An Interpretation
by Samuel S. Marquis

I have known Henry Ford for twenty years. For a time he was my parishioner, and then for a time I was his employee. (p. 4)

I once preached a sermon for Henry Ford's special benefit. I told him I was going to do so and asked him to be present and hear it. He came. He listened very attentively. He went away. It was a good sermon, if I do say so myself, but so far as I was ever able to see it never fazed him. (p. 80)

Mrs. Ford does much through the regular channels of the church and charity organizations. To her personal interest and wise guidance, the Ford hospital owes more than the public will ever know. To her generosity the Williams House, a church institution and a temporary home for border-line girls, owes its establishment. There are many who could speak as recipients of her private and individual charity. (p. 86)

But to return to Mr. Ford and the church. Frequently are the questions asked, "Is he a churchman?" "Is he a Christian?" "What are his religious views?" "Is he a religious man?" Mr. Ford was baptized and confirmed in the Episcopal Church. (p. 88)

His father was a vestryman in the little Episcopal church in Dearborn. It was in this church that Mr. Ford was baptized and confirmed. (p. 90)

On Charity

Mr. Ford hates the word charity and all that it stands for. (p. 104)

Mr. Ford has no use for the ordinary channels of charity and philanthropy. Such matters are taken care of by other members of the family. To the Red Cross, the Community Fund, the people destitute on account of sickness or the infirmity of years, and to many charitable institutions Mrs. Ford and Edsel give generously. (p. 104-105)

Over one thousand seven hundred cripples were in the employ of the company at the outbreak of the war. In addition to these, some four or five thousand more men, disabled more or less by disease, and who for that reason, would be rejected by industry, were on its payroll. After the war the company agreed to take a thousand handicapped men as fast as they came out of the hospitals. (p. 111)

He decries charity. He makes no attempt to conceal the fact. He believes that money should be made to work, and that men should work for money. He insists that anything that can't pay its own way has no right to exist. (p. 117)

The requests for money coming into his own office average, so I have been informed, over six million dollars a month. (p. 105)

Today and Tomorrow
by Henry Ford

It is clear up to them now, as trustees, (conservatives in charge of economic machinery vs. radicals who focus on adversity and criticism) to show what they can do further in the way of making our system foolproof, malice-proof, and greed-proof for the benefit of every person in the land. It is a mere matter of social engineering. It may have the effect of reducing "personal fortunes," but it will not have the effect of reducing working capital. What right has a "personal fortune" to be anything but working capital? The time is here when the commanding law is, "to whom much is given, of him much shall be required." (p. 238)

My Life and Work
by Henry Ford

There are many kinds of knowledge, and it depends on what crowd you happen to be in, or how the fashions of the day happen to run, which kind of knowledge is most respected at the moment. There are fashions in knowledge, just as there are in everything else. When some of us were lads, knowledge used to be limited to the Bible. There were certain men in the neighborhood who knew the Book thoroughly, and they were looked to and respected. Biblical knowledge was highly valued then. But now adays it is doubtful whether deep acquaintance with the Bible would be sufficient to win a man a name for learning. (p. 248)

The genius of the United States of America is Christian in the broadest sense, and its destiny is to remain Christian. This carries no sectarian meaning with it but relates to a basic principle which differs from other principles in that it provides for liberty with morality, and pledges society to a code of relations based on fundamental Christian conceptions of human rights and duties. As for prejudice or hatred against persons, that is neither American nor Christian. Our opposition is only to ideas, false ideas, which are sapping the moral stamina of the people. (p. 251)

Written in 1922

A great many things are going to change. We shall learn to be masters rather than servants of Nature. With all our fancied skill we still depend largely on natural resources and think that they cannot be displaced. We dig coal and ore and cut down trees. We use the coal and ore and they are gone; the trees cannot be replaced within a lifetime. We shall someday harness the heat that is all about us and no longer depend on coal—we may now create heat through electricity generated by water power. We shall improve on that method. As chemistry advances I feel quite certain that a method will be found to transform growing things into substances that will endure better than the metals—we have scarcely

147

touched the uses of cotton. Better wood can be made than is grown. The Spirit of true service will create for us.

We have only each of us to do our parts sincerely. Everything is possible... "faith is the substance of things hoped for, the evidence of things not seen." (p. 280-281)

Recommended Reading

On Andrew Carnegie

Alderson, Barnard. *Andrew Carnegie: The Man and His Work*. New York: Doubleday, Page & Co., 1902.

Carnegie, Andrew; Helps, Sir Arthur. *How to Win a Fortune. The Transaction of Business*. Madison: Eddy Publishing Company, 1904.

Carnegie, Andrew. *The Gospel of Wealth*. Belford: Applewood Books, 1998. (Reprint)

Henderson, Daniel. *Louise Whitfield Carnegie: The Life of Mrs. Andrew Carnegie*. New York 22: Hastings House, 1950.

On Henry Ford

Bryan, Ford R. *Friends Families & Forays: Scenes from Life and Times of Henry Ford*. Dearborn, Michigan: Ford Books, 2002.

Fay, Charles Norman. *Social Justice: The Moral of the Henry Ford Fortune*. Cambridge, Mass: The Cosmos Press, 1926.

Ford, Henry. *My Philosophy of Industry*. New York: Coward-McCann, Inc., 1929.

Marquis, Samuel S. *Henry Ford: An Interpretation*. Boston: Little Brown, and Company, 1923.

On J.P. Morgan

Allen, Frederick Lewis. *The Great Pierpont Morgan*. New York: Harper & Brothers, 1949.

Govenar, Alan; Maack, Mary Niles. *Anne Morgan: Photography, Philanthropy, & Advocacy.* New York: The American Friends of Blerancourt, 2016.

Hovey, Carl. *The Life Story of J. Pierpont Morgan*. London: William Heinemann, 1912.

Satterlee, Herbert L. *J. Pierpont Morgan.* New York: The MacMillan Company, 1939.

On John D. Rockefeller, Sr

Carr, Albert Z. *John D. Rockefeller's Secret Weapon*. New York, Toronto, London: McGraw-Hill Book Company, Inc., 1962.

Chernow, Ron. *Titan: The Life of John D. Rockefeller Sr.* New York: Random House, 1998.

Goulder, Grace. *John D. Rockefeller: The Cleveland Years.* Cleveland: The Western Reserve Historical Society, 1972.

Loebl, Suzanne. *America's Medics: The Rockefellers and Their Astonishing Cultural Legacy.* New York: Harper Collins Publishers, 2010.

On Cornelius Vanderbilt

Croffut, W.A. *The Vanderbilts and the Story of their Fortune*. Chicago and New York: Belford, Clarke & Company, 1886.

Lane, Wheaton J. *Commodore Vanderbilt: An Epic of the Steam Age.* New York: Alfred A. Knopf, 1942.

MacDowell, Dorothy Kelly. *Commodore Vanderbilt and His Family.* Hendersonville, NC: Dorothy K. MacDowell, 1989.

Vanderbilt II, Arthur T. *Fortune's Children: The Fall of the House of Vanderbilt.* Norwalk, Connecticut: The Easton Press, 1993.